William Pitt, Earl of Chatham, by William Hoare

MAKERS OF HISTORY

CHATHAM

by

J. H. PLUMB

Archon Books

HAMDEN, CONNECTICUT

1965

First published in 1953
First published in the 'Makers of History' Series 1965

To
YVONNE AND ANTHONY
DE ROTHSCHILD
in gratitude

Library of Congress Catalog Card number
65-19159

Contents

Plates

Maps

* 1 *

The Cornet of Horse

ON FEBRUARY 20th, 1682, a small fleet of trading vessels hurriedly left the Thames. They carried with them Lord Chatham's grandfather, who had been forbidden to leave the country. Letters were immediately despatched by the Governors of the East India Company to warn their agents in India of this ' fellow of a haughty, huffying daring temper.' He was to be arrested at once; and 'when you have got him into your custody be sure secure him, he being a desperate fellow and one that we fear will not stick at doing any mischief that lies in his power.' There was no arrest. Thomas Pitt made rings round the Company. He raced their ships to India, collected a private army of Portuguese and half-castes which scared the Company's servants into respectful caution, and carried on a roaring trade which was so profitable that he was able to leave seven months later with a fortune. This was the second fortune he had made in India through resolute and violent action and in defiance of the power and authority of the Company. He was just thirty years of age. Yet, in the end, it was the Company which had to make peace with Pitt. In 1698 he was appointed Governor of their finest factory, Fort St. George, at Madras. There his name became a byword for outrageous temper, but trade flourished and British power grew stronger. Nor did Governor Pitt neglect his own pocket. He dabbled in diamonds and risked £25,000 on one of the largest stones ever discovered in India. It took him thirteen years to get the price which he thought it was worth. But in 1717 he sold it for £133,000 to the Regent of France.

The ownership of land and the control of seats in Parliament were the ways rich merchants bought themselves a place in society and government during the eighteenth century. And they followed it up, if they could, with the marriage of their children into the aristocracy. As Pitt had made his fortunes, so he had laid out his money in this way, buying the estate of Boconnoc in Cornwall for £53,000 and many other properties in Dorset, Berkshire and London. He also obtained complete control of the rotten borough of Old Sarum, which returned two members of Parliament; his power at Okehampton, a Devon borough, was almost as great. And he saw his children married into aristocratic families. Yet it all had a bitter taste for Governor Pitt. His wealth, acquired with such resolution, was squandered by his extravagant children. He quarrelled with his wife. He loathed his sons and daughters—'the cockatrice brood of Pitts' as he called them. In his family all was rage and violence and hate.

Already in India Governor Pitt had been notorious for the ferocity of his temper. His language could acquire an apocalyptic fury which burnt itself into men's memories. The smouldering fire of his temperament flashed out in all his actions. At times he seemed poised on the brink of insanity. Men deferred to him, subordinates feared him. To the very end of his days he was ignorant of friendship, ignorant of the warmth and ease of life. Then suddenly the heart of this stark, terrifying character was touched by one of his grandchildren, William Pitt. Whenever he could he sent over to Eton from his house at Swallowfield to fetch the boy and his ' comrogues.' The long afternoons passed quietly with tales of Indian adventure. The old man lived again the tempestuous scenes of his youth and taught his young listener that trade and wealth could be won only by risk and violence, a lesson which Pitt was never to forget. " He is a hopeful lad," Governor Pitt wrote to his father, " and doubt not but that he will answer yours and all his friends' expectations." The old man was right to be proud, for, by his grandson, his attitude to life was to be exalted into a nation's creed. Yet from his grandfather Pitt derived a dark inheritance.

William Pitt had been born on November 15th, 1708, at Golden Square, London. He was sent to Eton at the age of ten, but was so intensely miserable there that he refused to send any of his children to school. From Eton he proceeded to Trinity College, Oxford. He flirted with the idea of entering the Church, for, as a younger son, it was essential for him to have a profession. Governor Pitt's ' cursed brood ' were wolfishly devouring the magnificent inheritance which he had left them. There were to be no crumbs for Pitt. After abandoning the idea of the Church, Pitt found Oxford distasteful. Restlessly he moved to Utrecht which he found no more congenial than Oxford, for he was soon back at Boconnoc, the great estate in Cornwall, which his grandfather had bought from the profits of the diamond. There he read and idled away his time, sometimes quarrelling with his family but always doting on his favourite sister, Ann. His elder brother Thomas Lyttelton of Hagley, a leading figure in a large political connection whose leader, Viscount Cobham, lived in superb ostentation at his vast palace of Stowe in Buckinghamshire. A morsel of patronage came Pitt's way. He was made in January, 1731, a cornet in the Second or King's Own Regiment of Horse of which Cobham was colonel. The pay was small but welcome, and the duties so light that Pitt was able two years later to make a short tour abroad.

Pitt was twenty-six. He had given little sign of genius or of ambition. He moved aloof on the fringe of society and politics. But in 1735 a vacancy occurred at the family borough of Old Sarum. William Pitt took the proffered opportunity and entered Parliament. Before the beginning of his first sessions, he spent the summer at Stowe. There were gathered the great men of the opposition—Cobham, Pulteney, Chesterfield, Bolton—the great lords whom Walpole had forced from office and degraded.

In the gracious gardens of Stowe men dreamed of revenge. Pitt listened in silence to the bitter and

venomous wit of Chesterfield and the satirical eloquence
of Pulteney. He learned how Walpole was betraying
the interests of England; selling her cheap to France
and Spain; an old man fearful of war, fearful of
losing the confidence of the King, and with it the
patronage and the power which had made him for
nearly twenty years the greatest man in England.
Their words of hatred echoed in Pitt's heart. So his
grandfather had spoken. Hate, as Pitt knew, was an
exaltation, releasing the violence which tortured his
lonely heart. That summer at Stowe brought Pitt and
his destiny together. In his first speeches in the
Commons there is an intoxication, a note of frenzy, a
concentration of emotional force elemental in its
power. His listeners were lost in admiration or fear.
Walpole acted decisively. He threw Pitt out of his
army commission. " We must muzzle," he said,
" this terrible cornet of the horse." As well might he
attempt to stop a hurricane with a hair net.

But this is to run too fast. Something must be said
both of Pitt's character and of the world of politics
into which he was launched. Firstly, his character.
Much is obvious from his career and need not be
described, but there is a darker side about which
plain speaking is necessary. From time to time Pitt
was mad. In technical terms he was a manic-depressive.
This means that the tempo of his life would begin to
quicken; with gathering momentum, exaltation, sense
of power, visionary insight, prophetic frenzy, a furious
concentration of will would fuse until he felt like God
turning the world with His finger tip. Then suddenly

his soaring spirits would plunge; despair, as dark a despair as any can know, would follow, unendurable in its intensity. The only recourse was retreat to the lonely recesses of the heart where no human voice could reach.

These phases of madness were intermittent. They built up at first slowly and in their early stages gave a heightened intensity to all that Pitt said or did, yet probably he gained rather than lost from them, for they gave his utterances a compellingly oracular and prophetic note. But the aftermath of despair was a grave handicap. Because there was no knowledge of his disease it was not so grave a handicap as it would be at the present time. Now it would be impossible for anyone who suffered as Pitt suffered to remain long in political life. Pitt and his family were aware of his weakness; euphemistically it was called gout in the head. Actually Pitt did suffer from gout and it was thought that the two diseases were associated. But Pitt also built up another defence. He created an artificial personality in which he could hide. He became elaborately formal, unknowable, ostentatiously acting the great man of affairs; thus he kept the world at a distance, kept it from seeing the terrifying cracks which fissured his personality. When the days were radiant the rôle suited him to perfection for the delusion of grandeur acquired reality. When the storm began to rage within, what might have seemed fantastic from any other man no longer seemed unusual from Pitt, because the world was attuned to the loftiness of his regard.

And finally, his madness had a most important political value; it gave an edge, a divine frenzy, to his oratory which made all who listened to him feel that Chatham was but the mouthpiece of destiny; that his politics were related to the drama of mankind and not associated with the sordid considerations of personal power and party manœuvre. It meant that his words had greater authority than other men's, although his actions were less calculable.

When Pitt entered Parliament in 1735, Walpole had ruled England since 1720. He was a hard-working, hard-headed Norfolk man who was extremely clever at handling men. He was particularly good at smelling out a dangerous rival, and any politician who tried to undermine Walpole's influence with King George II or his Queen, Caroline, soon found himself out of office.

In the early eighteenth century there were no party organisations as we know them. Men were labelled Whig or Tory but it meant very little; factions were much more important. Factions were groups of politicians tied to each other by family or territorial loyalties; men who had decided to strive for power together. These factions, when in power, made certain that all offices great or small went to those prepared to support them. But men quickly learned to love the emoluments of their offices more than their masters, and all governments had an exhausting and anxious time keeping their followers quiet and devoted. Walpole was quite masterly at this type of political management. He knew by instinct when to use the bribe and when to use the threat. Also, in the Duke of Newcastle he had a lieutenant who was willing to spend all of his time and most of his fortune in political jobbery so long as he could cut a figure of importance at the Court. His long continuance in power had made Walpole a number of furious enemies—the witty and able men Pitt listened to at Stowe. They detested his corrupt methods and denounced them in their newspaper, *The Craftsman*.

This attitude particularly pleased the Tories. They hated London, the Court, place-holders, pensioners, long Parliaments and corrupt elections where their shortage of money lost them seats. But the more intelligent and far-sighted members of the opposition were not worried overmuch by Walpole's corruption. They knew as well as he did that it was the only way to make politics work without a radical reform of the constitution—which was unthinkable. They had a graver charge against him, and one which carried great weight with the merchants of London. They accused Walpole of buying peace at too dear a price.

Walpole's aims had always been simple; peace, low taxation, efficient financial methods. He was often impatient of difficulties in foreign affairs. He compromised willingly and seemed indifferent to national pride. For years England hovered on the brink of war with Spain. Late in the seventeenth century English merchants had begun to build up a secret trade with the Spanish colonies in America, a trade which Spain itself would not tolerate. At the Treaty of Utrecht

*Plate 1.   Thomas Pitt, Governor of Fort St. George, Madras
by Van der Bank*

Plate 2. Thomas Holles, 1st Duke of Newcastle
by William Hoare

in 1713 Britain had forced Spain to legitimise this trade or rather a token of this trade. By the Assiento clauses, in addition to a modest trade in slaves, one ship a year, full of merchandise, was allowed to trade in the West Indies. This may have been a mortification to Spanish pride, but it was a trivial concession to the English merchants. And, of course, it was ignored; ships slipped across from Jamaica and the sugar islands to the Spanish main.

For a long time the Spaniards connived at this for they needed the goods which the English merchants brought to sell. But the Spanish government deplored this development and set up a system of coastguards to trap English ships. Some of these coastguards behaved more like pirates than naval officers, but then many Englishmen behaved more like smugglers than merchants. Tempers grew short and violence ensued. In 1731 a pamphlet was issued in London setting out the brutalities suffered by our traders. It proved popular and there followed a steady stream of anti-Spanish propaganda from the press. London merchants petitioned the King for support. To many men it seemed insufferable that a second-rate Power like Spain should inflict indignities on Englishmen and that they should exclude merchants from the rich West Indian trade.

Many saw behind this Spanish attitude the sinister hand of France, our greatest European rival. Walpole had kept on very friendly terms with France. Many considered him to be the dupe of the astute French Minister, Cardinal Fleury. The opposition denounced

C.   B

Walpole's policy as a national humiliation. The real
force and power of the opposition was derived from
this intense hatred which the city merchants felt
towards the government's foreign policy. Naturally
they opposed Walpole on many questions but this was
the heart of the matter.

It was an attitude to which Pitt was instinctively
drawn, an attitude certainly to which his grandfather
would have given ardent support. It was not Spain,
however, which first drew Walpole's attention to Pitt.
As a member of the opposition he had supported the
Prince of Wales's demand for marriage and a fixed
allowance of £100,000 a year. Although the Prince
was of age he had been kept dependent on the King
for he was hated by his father and mother with a fury
which made old Pitt seem amiable. Naturally the
Prince turned to the opposition, where he was more
than welcome for the intransigence of the royal attitude
gave great scope for agitation. After a year's delay
the King married the Prince to Princess Augusta of
Saxe-Gotha. Pitt made a notable speech on the
congratulatory address which the Commons presented
to the King. It was a masterpiece of sarcastic insinua-
tion. It irritated Walpole sufficiently to make him
use his whip. Lord Cobham had recently been dismissed his regiment for opposition. It was a warning
to be heeded by his subordinates. By this speech Pitt
showed that he had no intention of curbing his tongue
or changing his views. He was cashiered. But for once
Walpole mistook his man, or at least underestimated
him. With typical ostentation Pitt drove about

London in a one-horse chaise to underline his poverty, which was real enough, for his total income was no more than three hundred a year. And Pitt brooded revenge.

He did not have long to wait. Anglo-Spanish relations floundered from bad to worse. In February, 1738, Captain Jenkins with his famous ear, severed by the Spaniards in 1731 and kept conveniently in a bottle of spirits ever since, was presented to the Commons as evidence of the brutality which our sailors and merchants suffered. Newcastle became convinced that war was necessary, and he forced Walpole to more aggressive action. A fleet was sent to the Mediterranean and a regiment to Georgia. The tone in despatches to Madrid hardened. Spain offered to negotiate, an offer which Walpole seized at once. After protracted negotiations the Convention of Pardo was signed on January 3rd, 1739. The opposition received it with derision. They regarded the trivial compensation offered by the Spaniards to our merchants as a national disgrace. When the Government moved to address the King, thanking him for having achieved the Convention, the debate in the Commons became violent and bitter. Pitt waited for the debate to grow warm and spoke seventh. It was the best speech of his early career and established his reputation as the greatest orator of his time. Even now there is tremendous force and vigour in some of the phrases he is known to have used.

" When Trade is at stake, you must defend it or

perish . . . You are moved to thank for a measure odious, and I appeal to the breast of every gentleman. You throw out general terrors of war. Spain knows the consequences of war in America, but she sees England dare not make it. . . . This Convention, Sir, I think upon my Soul is nothing but a stipulation of national ignominy; an illusory expedient, to baffle the resentment of the nation; a truce without a suspension of hostilities on the part of Spain; on the part of England . . . a surrender of the rights and trade of England to the mercy of plenipotentiaries . . . The complaints of your despairing merchants— the voice of England—has condemned it."[1]

Although Walpole survived the debate by a narrow majority, he was in the end driven into war. " Your war," as he bitterly told the Duke of Newcastle, " and I wish you joy of it." Little joy was to be had of it, for years of peace and short commons had brought the navy and the army to a low ebb. No strenuous exertions were made by Walpole to improve conditions. Baffled and irritated, the opposition pursued Walpole from session to session with bitter hatred and contempt. The old man clung desperately to office, hoping that time which had so often saved him would save him now. But the friends of a life-time indicated their readiness to collaborate with the more moderate sections of the opposition, and Walpole could no longer carry on.

[1] Quotations of his speech are derived partly from the *Parliamentary History* and partly from notes taken at the debate by Sir Dudley Ryder, now in the possession of the Earl of Harrowby, who has kindly allowed me to use them. The two versions agree in substance.

The young patriots, of whom Pitt was the most vociferous and the most venomous in his attacks, wanted not Walpole's retirement but his ruin. They fought for his impeachment and secured by a narrow majority an inquiry into his administration. Pitt managed to obtain a seat on the Committee which was ordered to carry out the investigation. A large volume of notes testifies to the eagerness with which Pitt undertook his duties. But Walpole's servants were too loyal and Pitt was thwarted.

In his final onslaught on the minister, Pitt had shown little judgment, no capacity to curb the violence of his feelings, no willingness to moderate his furious need for revenge. Passions as naked as his are the staff of life to men in opposition, but they breed no confidence in a capacity to rule. As is usual in political crises of a secondary order, it was the moderate, cautious, compromising men on both sides with whom the victory rested; Cobham's cubs had no share in the spoils.

There was nothing for Pitt to regret. Throughout the struggle he had spoken with honest conviction, reckless of the consequences. By so doing he had lifted the debate beyond a sordid struggle for power. The question had been asked, and once asked it could not be forgotten. What was to be England's future ? Was she to destroy Spain and France and seize the commerce of the world? This was the intoxicating prospect which Pitt offered to his countrymen; he avowed what they hoped but dared not utter; wealth, grandeur, an empire greater than the world had known since Rome. The government politicians dismissed his speeches as 'formidable sounds and furious declamation,' but to men of his grandfather's stamp they were words of destiny.

* 2 *

Years of Frustration

PITT WAS denied power. His popularity in London
was greater than that of any statesman of his time.
He had, more than any other man, created that atmos-
phere of distrust and rage which had helped to bring
about Walpole's fall. Yet his attack on the government's policy had been too uncompromising for him to
be able to barter for place. With all the recklessness of
his nature he had risked all on being right. According
to Pitt, any policy which did not lead to out-and-out
war with France and Spain for control of the world's
trade would only bring misery, frustration and disaster
to Britain. And to achieve this a total effort by the
nation would be needed. Half-hearted measures,
reliance on dubious allies and mercenaries, could never
bring the victory for which Pitt so passionately longed.
He was so certain of this that he was prepared to stake
his career on it.

Although men in the City were certain that he was
right, men at Westminster were more doubtful. Certainty of conviction, resolutely held, is always a
dangerous attitude for a politician; so is a policy of
risk. Politicians prefer the comfortable, conforming

ways of half-measures. It is easier to let the ship of state drift on the tide. Only when the rocks loom up and disaster is near, will they trust men of authority and adventure. This has been true of the greatest statesmen of our century—Lloyd George and Winston Churchill—and it was true of William Pitt.

It was expected by men unschooled in politics that the fall of Walpole would lead to an intensification of the war against Spain. Nothing of the sort happened. He was succeeded by Lord Wilmington, whose Cabinet was dominated by Carteret, a wealthy nobleman of high intelligence but little energy, a man who loved the splendours of diplomacy and loathed the drudgery of politics. " What is it to me," he is reputed to have said, " who is a judge or a bishop? It is my business to make kings and emperors, and to maintain the balance of Europe." Unfortunately, on the day Carteret entered office there was a tangled web of diplomatic affairs awaiting his attention.

The war in which England was engaged had begun as a war against Spain, but in October, 1740, Charles VI, the Emperor of the Holy Roman Empire, and ruler of the vast Hapsburg territories in Austria, Hungary, Bohemia, Italy and the Low Countries, died. His heir was his daughter, Maria Theresa, and although she could not, being a woman, succeed to the Empire, she inherited the Hapsburg dominions. Before his death Charles had obtained a solemn guarantee from all European powers (the Pragmatic Sanction) that she would be allowed to do so. Yet within two months of his death Frederick of Prussia had invaded Silesia,

Hapsburg territory, claiming it as his own. Frederick did not lack imitators. The Elector of Bavaria demanded parts of Bohemia and Austria. The sons of the Spanish Queen, Elizabeth Farnese, asserted their rights to the Hapsburg lands in Northern Italy, and they were backed by Spanish arms. France extended her benevolent support to the enemies of Austria; Holland took refuge in neutrality; England alone honoured her engagements under the Pragmatic Sanction, for a formidable increase in Bourbon power was not to be tolerated. But Walpole restricted his help to the provision of 12,000 mercenary troops from Hesse and Denmark, together with a great deal of contradictory advice. As his loyal old brother, Horace, lamented, "We have no great plan in view; we act by fits and starts."

When Carteret took office the French were at the gates of Vienna. He plunged into the situation with relish. He raised Maria Theresa's subsidy; cajoled her into making peace with Frederick so that she could the more easily withstand the French. A British squadron in the Bay of Naples quickly stopped the ambitions of the Spanish princes. But for Carteret this was small beer. A great army was conjured forth in the Low Countries under the choleric command of Lord Stair, aged seventy. Money was poured into the pockets of the German princes in return for their mercenaries, but Englishmen were astonished to find that they were paying their own King for 16,000 of his Hanoverian troops. They paid him, of course, not as King of England but as Elector of Hanover. Nor had

Carteret bothered to ask for the consent of Parliament, a fact which Pitt was quick to seize on. But even worse for Carteret, Stair, who chafed to be at the gate of Paris, was thwarted by the failure of the Dutch to provide troops. The army wintered in idleness. A situation upon which Pitt poured withering scorn.

" Neither justice nor policy," he fumed, " required us to be engaged in the quarrels of the Continent . . . the confidence of the people is abused by making unnecessary alliances ; they are then pillaged to provide the subsidies. It is now too apparent that this great, this powerful, this formidable kingdom is considered only as a province of a despicable electorate."

Carteret, according to Pitt, was entangled in his own diplomacy, which had become so intricate that the purpose of England's entry into the war had been obscured. England's need was to fight Spain and wrest trading privileges from her: if France came to the aid of her ally, then France should be fought, but not in Europe. That was folly. France should be fought like Spain on the seas and in her far-distant trading posts of India and America. These were Pitt's convictions.

He had been making a close study of France's economy, of its trade and manufacture and also of its maritime strength. He was appalled by what he learned. In the long years of friendship which had been established by Walpole, France had been steadily building up her navy until it had reached formidable proportions. To waste our small reserves in useless continental campaigns seemed suicidal to Pitt. The only reason, he felt, which could explain such a singular act of folly was a desire to gratify the King, for as Elector of Hanover he was naturally concerned with the safety of his German dominions. Hence the cry that a great Kingdom was being sacrificed for a petty German state.

King George was infuriated. He found the English difficult enough, he hated the ' damned House of Commons ' and his loathing of Pitt knew no bounds. Although Pitt's invective delighted the nation, for they hated foreigners, especially Germans, yet his chance of office became more remote. The King regarded him as a personal enemy, and the King had the deciding voice in the choice of his ministers; and in consequence his prejudices carried great weight. The situation did not improve when Pitt sneered at George II's military prowess. At Dettingen in 1743, the King had led his troops forward, sword in hand, and by this act of courage he had rallied the army and helped to bring about a French defeat. But through weak generalship, the allied forces had failed to take advantage of the disorder of the French troops. It was easy for Pitt to belittle the importance of Dettingen and explode the bubble reputation which the King had enjoyed when the first reports of the battle were given in the London press.

This enmity in which the King held Pitt was disastrous, but there were politicians who thought that the King might be bullied or cajoled into taking Pitt into the government and that the risks and difficulties involved would be worth it. The chief of these was Henry Pelham, the brother of the Duke of Newcastle, who had been airily dismissed by Carteret as ' Sir Robert Walpole's chief clerk,' capable of drudgery but nothing more. Carteret, unfortunately for himself, was completely outmanœuvred by the man he despised, and when Wilmington, the titular head of the ministry, died, it was Pelham and not Carteret's protégé, Lord Bath, who became head of the ministry.

Pelham was subtle and dexterous, and he had the help of the subtler and more experienced hand of Sir Robert Walpole, now Earl of Orford, who advised Pelham to tackle Pitt. Pelham took Walpole's counsel and came to an understanding with Pitt. Carteret could be attacked as often and as fiercely as Pitt wished, but in return he was to support the presence of the army in the Low Countries, a concession which he found no difficulty in making, for their protection had long been a cardinal point of commercial policy— Pitt's former objection had been to a large and expensive army wandering about the frontiers of France without purpose.

This was a political manœuvre of great subtlety and the skilful hand of Walpole is clearly visible. It concentrated opposition on Carteret and it was Pelham's ultimate aim, of course, to get rid of him ; yet the sting of Pitt's opposition to the war was drawn and the road cleared for the creation of a government so widely based that all the important political factions would be tied to it. Walpole and Pelham hoped that the

ferocities of opposition would thereby be quelled and
the King's ministers rest secure in a large majority.
With rather heavy Hanoverian humour the wits
called this a Broad-bottomed Administration.

And so the Grenvilles and Pitt were ensnared by
men to whom the trickery of politics was second nature,
for by this pact Pelham was aided in his struggle with
Carteret, who was finally dismissed in November 1744.
The King hated parting with him. He sulked and
refused to give his full confidence to his new ministry,
so that Walpole was forced to write to him in very
blunt terms. " The present suspense is certain destruction of all your affairs both at home and abroad. For
God's sake, Sir, give the proper support and authority
to those in whose hands you have placed your Administration. . . . Any other method, at present, will but
increase the impracticability of all business; all new
attempts are new confusion."[1] The King was dis-
pleased and returned the letter unanswered, but
eventually he obeyed his old dictator. Carteret was
not brought back; Pelham was given full support. On
one question alone the King was immovable—Pitt
should have no office.

All the rest of his friends were ' in '—Chesterfield,
Cobham, Lyttelton and George Grenville. The Stowe
House group, after ten years of opposition, were
brought back to the comfort of emoluments. But,
Pitt, the greatest of them all, who by his insight and
his incomparable oratory had earned them their places,
was left to fend for himself. It was a bitter blow, for

[1] From the Cholmondeley (Houghton) MSS., not before printed.

Pitt ardently longed for the power which he felt his gifts merited. His oldest political friends had not stood firm for him. Nor was a renewed and vigorous opposition possible, for he could not join forces with Carteret, because of the bitterness between them, and everyone else of importance was in the government, so Pitt supported the ministry and hoped for the best. Pelham for his part honoured his agreement and Pitt had the satisfaction of seeing the policy which he had advocated—namely, the removal of Hanoverian troops from British pay-roll—carried out.

The voice which had thundered for nearly a decade against the government now became unctuous in its support. It was obvious to all that it could only be a matter of time before Pitt was brought into the ministry. Pelham was able to force the King's hand in 1746. Our armies had been beaten in France and the country was in the throes of a Jacobite rebellion. At this carefully chosen time Pelham made his bid : either Pitt was to be given office or the ministry would resign. George denounced Pelham and let him resign, but he failed to get any other politician to form a government. Pop-eyed with rage, the King was forced to give way, but he conceded as little as he could for he flatly refused to have Pitt as Secretary at War, the office upon which he had set his heart. As Secretary, George would have been forced to see him regularly; and that was too much to be borne. Pitt had to content himself with an office of standing and no power—namely, the Paymastership of the Forces, an office which rarely brought him into the royal presence.

Pelham had fixed Pitt. There can be no doubt that he had been completely outmanœuvred; a view held by many of his supporters who, sad and bewildered, read the lampoons and caricatures which poured from the press. In the coffee-houses the ballad girls sang of his disgrace.

> " *He bellow'd and roar'd at the troops of Hanover,*
> *And swore they were rascals whoever went over;*
> *That no man was honest who gave them a vote,*
> *And all that were for 'em should hang by the throat.*
>
> *Whilst Balaam was poor, he was full of renown,*
> *But now that he's rich, he's the jest of the town :*
> *Then let all men learn by his present disgrace*
> *That honesty's better by far than a place.*"

Was it, after all, mere sound and fury? Did he lack all heroic quality? Was he merely an actor, a poseur? In 1746 it looked as if it were so. Men deeply versed in political life congratulated Pitt. They thought that they recognised sound political tactics for they assumed that Pitt had pursued such a violent, anti-government policy in order to drive up his price. The fact that Pitt had won the most profitable place in the ministry seemed to justify their interpretation. Little did they know their man.

We must go back to 1744 and remember Pitt's character, its instabilities and dangers. It is in the nature of a manic-depressive to be able to throw away quite casually all that has formerly concentrated his attention and ambition. In that year Pitt fell ill, partly with the gout, but in the main he suffered from a mental collapse. He was troubled with continuous insomnia and great irritation of the nerves. The Cobham group were very worried, and George Grenville wrote to his brother: " Pitt is . . . in a very bad way. The Bath waters have done him no good. This is a grievous misfortune to him, since, if it does not affect his life, it may perhaps disable him." And months later, in January, 1745, the French Ambassador who saw him enter the Commons thought that he was dying. This was Pitt's state throughout the critical negotiations which led to the formation of the Broad-bottomed Administration and to his final acceptance of office. The timing of Pelham's dextrous manœuvre to trap Pitt could not have been more perfect, for when he needed all his intellectual powers unimpaired he was entangled in the horrors of his temperament.

In the depths of his depression he must have considered his life. For nine years he had struggled to destroy his enemies and win through to political power. He was thirty-seven, unmarried, almost penniless. In his exhaustion and despair much of his struggle must have seemed useless. A new tack meant new hope. Once in office, his gifts would be recognised. If he rejected his chance, he would be alone in opposition with no one to sustain him, alone maybe for years, all chance of leading his country lost. Also, in his state, the surface glitter of office would attract him, fascinate his attention, and draw away his concentration from his darker self.

This need for concentration outside himself was also

one of the reasons why it helped him to make such a public parade of his illness. His enemies, particularly young Horace Walpole, poured scorn on Pitt's paraphernalia—the crutches, the huge boot for his gouty foot, the swathes of bandages, with which he appeared in the Commons—for the first time, be it noted, in January, 1745. Apart from arousing public sympathy, the more the foot was in evidence, the less gossip there was about the head. But the real help arose because when he was acting the sick and dying man all his attention was required and he could not brood. And so office too might be a continuous distraction; work would prevent him thinking. It was not to be the last time Pitt was to bewilder his public by a sudden turnabout, but whenever he did it usually arose from a personal crisis and was a corollary of his disease.

But Pitt had one stroke of luck with his acceptance of office; it happened after the death of Sarah, Duchess of Marlborough, the widow of the great Marlborough. She was a turbulent old woman with a temper as ferocious as old Governor Pitt's; indeed she was so violent that her nickname in society was 'Mount Etna.' For her Walpole was an incarnation of evil bent on destroying all the benefits which her husband's victories had won for England. The words of Pitt were balm to the old woman and when she died in August, 1744, she left him a legacy of £10,000 and made him co-heir presumptive to half of her great estates. For the first time in his life Pitt acquired a modest affluence and considerable prospects. They were both put to excellent use.

* 3 *

Paymaster-General

WITHOUT A doubt Pitt had disappointed his public by becoming Paymaster-General of the Forces. Almost any other place would have seemed less disastrous than this, for there were some strange customs associated with the office. Each year the huge sums required to pay the army were handed over to the Paymaster; many months later the bills came in, but, until they did, the Paymaster was at liberty to do whatever he liked with the money. If he invested it, and made a profit, then the profit was his. So long as the bills were ultimately paid, and the accounts squared, the government was satisfied. As accountants were always twenty or thirty years behind the times, Paymasters could be certain of having many thousands of pounds with which to speculate.

Naturally it was regarded as the most lucrative of offices. After a period of opposition Walpole refused to accept the office of Chancellor of the Exchequer on the grounds that he could not afford it, or as Sir Robert bluntly put it, ' he was thin and needed to get some fat on his bones,' so instead he became Paymaster of the Forces. He thrived so well that he was able to resign within twelve months and take on the Chancellor-ship. Another profitable sideline of the Paymaster's was the gifts which he received every time a subsidy was made to a foreign prince or when mercenary troops were hired. In fact all Paymasters had made immense fortunes. So Pitt had not only accepted an office, but an office notorious even in the eighteenth century for its perquisites. For a man who had been vociferous in his denunciation of corruption it was a singular choice. Naturally enough, the hack-writers and the gossips called Pitt a hypocrite and the majority of men believed them.

They were wrong. Pitt was neither a hypocrite nor a fool. To have accepted the perquisites of his office would have destroyed his public fame. Pitt knew that well enough, so he refused them, not quietly and unobtrusively but with ostentatious publicity. Pitt had lost favour and he wanted to regain it. He osten-tatiously lodged his balances with the Bank of England for the public use. It was a master-stroke. The relation between a statesman and the public is often highly emotional and very unstable. And this dramatic act of Pitt's immediately wiped out the sense of betrayal which many had felt at his taking office. His enemies and near friends were cynical; to them it was just another of Pitt's theatrical gestures, designed to dupe the public. It would be foolish to deny that his action had a touch of the theatre and that Pitt was in no way averse to the praise which it brought. But it was more than that. Pitt had a lofty spirit. Money meant little to him, and attachment to it he despised as a weakness; for years he had lived on £300 a year and cadged his holidays in his friends' country houses, and he did this at a time when a more accommodating spirit might have brought him a fortune. Nor could it have been easy for a poor man to throw away riches. His legacy from Sarah and the bright prospects of her inheritance may have strengthened his resolution. Yet, when all is said, this remains: Pitt alone of eighteenth-century statesmen made this gesture.

The years which followed his acceptance of office were the most peaceful years of Pitt's life. His work as Paymaster entranced him. He mastered its detail and he kept in close personal contact with his agents abroad, an innovation which his subordinates appreciated. Yet hard as he worked, he still had leisure. The House of Commons made little drain on his time. He was content with Pelham and Pelham's policy. When he was needed he spoke with all his old fire and eloquence, so much so that he even earned the grudging admiration of the King, but not being often needed, he had time to spare. He was not idle. The concentration of work was an anodyne to a man of his temperament. Even when he was in opposition he had begun to study with great thoroughness the commercial statistics of France. Now he had greater facilities, better material from confidential reports of our agents and from discussions with our representatives overseas. He was able to work out in detail his ideas on empire, trade and strategy. This was of the greatest importance, for when he was later called to the supreme power, he knew exactly what he wanted to do.

It was these studies which brought Pitt into touch with the more aggressive and vigorous merchants of the City of London, men of his grandfather's stamp. The rough, coarse-mannered William Beckford must have reminded Pitt strongly of Governor Pitt. He had the same forceful way of speaking and acting, the same passionate belief in England's mercantile capacity. They became close friends and Pitt learned from Beckford about the nature of our West Indian trade, of the seriousness of French competition, of the desirability of freeing the Spanish main from trade restrictions. Frequently they discussed the best strategy to pursue in time of war, arguing the merits of capturing the French sugar islands, which Pitt thought would wound France and benefit England, but about which Beckford had his doubts. From 1746 onwards Pitt was also in correspondence with William Vaughan, an American fish merchant of New Hampshire, whose imagination had been fired by the capture of Louisburg, the French citadel at the mouth of the great St. Lawrence river. Vaughan argued that the victory should be followed up by an attack on Quebec, the key to Canada. Pitt was convinced and he tried to persuade his colleagues in the ministry, Bedford and Newcastle, but they were fearful of the cost; already the expense of the war was worrying members of Parliament, for the tax on land was heavy. Another merchant, the Quaker Cumming, taught Pitt the value of the African trade to France. About India he required no lessons. But throughout these quiet years in office Pitt was deepening his knowledge, learning how trade could be made to flourish by war.

Pitt had other distractions apart from office, and the excitement of the paper campaigns fought with his new friends, for, although he refused the perquisites of his office, the salary attached to it was ample enough, about £4,000, for him to set up a household. Realising that much of his life might have to be spent at Bath, he began to build himself a house there. Whatever captured Pitt's attention received profound concentration, and it was not long before he was acknowledged amongst his friends as an expert on all problems relating to architecture and gardening. His letters on these matters are couched in the same authoritarian language in which he so frequently gave the Commons a lesson in politics.

And so all Pitt's time was taken up in new pursuits which brought fresh hope to his tortured personality. As year passed into year and the memory of the pain and horror of 1744 grew less, it seemed as if he might have won through to peace if not happiness.

The country, too, was steadily recovering from the disasters of 1745 when invasion at home and disaster abroad had created a momentary panic, but a salutary one. The critics of the Hanoverians had been bitter, cynical, careless of consequences, but the Young Pretender at Derby jolted them into a sense of reality. The prospect of civil war, of a restored monarchy with inherited attitudes inimical to the country's interests, killed Jacobitism stone dead, or rather turned it into a romantic frippery. The danger of a divided country which had lasted for nearly sixty years was over and at Culloden in 1746, England tore to pieces the fascination of her Stuart past. But Culloden could not win the war in Europe. In 1747, it is true, we managed to wrest supremacy at sea from France by the gallant actions of Anson off Finisterre and Hawke at Belleisle, victories which materially assisted our position in India where Madras had been lost and Dupleix triumphant. France was unable to reinforce her army in India, and in consequence the tables were turned on Dupleix, who was driven on to the defensive. But in Europe France was everywhere triumphant, so triumphant that Henry Pelham bewailed to his crony, old Horace Walpole, Sir Robert's brother: ' We fight all and pay all, it is true, but we are beaten and shall be broke '—an opinion which Pitt endorsed. He was apprehensive for the Dutch whose chief fortresses were endangered, and he had always been strongly in favour of peace with Frederick the Great of Prussia whom he admired. The destruction of the French fleet and the harrying effects of the cost of the war on her finances made France willing to negotiate; many Frenchmen thought too willing, for the Treaty of Aix-la-Chapelle, which was signed in 1748, gave rise to the saying, *bête comme la paix.*

By this treaty all conquests on both sides were restored and only Frederick, who was confirmed in his right to Silesia, gained anything. In effect Aix-la-Chapelle was to prove merely a truce. Not even a complete truce, for France and England continued to fight in India. To most men it was axiomatic that another war was but a matter of time. When it did come Pitt was determined that it should not be fought on the old system of a large continental army fighting side by side with the Austrians and the Dutch. He wanted to be on the side of Frederick the Great even if it meant breaking with Austria. George II might regard the King of Prussia as " a mischievous rascal and bad friend, a bad ally, a bad relation, and a bad neighbour, in fact the most dangerous and evil-disposed prince in Europe." But for Pitt he was Europe's salvation. He possessed the one army capable of curbing the growing power of France. During the years of peace Pitt was to press for the acceptance of these views. He made little progress, for the Duke of Newcastle, who was principally in charge of foreign policy, was obstinately wedded to the traditional alliances. His efforts were also hampered by a recurrence of his illness.

In 1751 Pitt alarmed his friends by an extravagant speech in the House of Commons in defence of an obscure family of Minorca whom he offered to defend with the last drop of his blood. His wild words were out of all proportion to the subject. Shortly afterwards he collapsed; gout, insomnia, nervous prostration followed. He knew again the utter despair from which he had struggled to free himself by radically changing the course of his life. For a time the new tack had worked. The interest of his work as Paymaster the delight in being in office with its frequent and serious consultations with men of affairs, all of these had proved sufficient distraction. His new wealth had provided other avenues of absorbing interest, enabling him to live in the splendour which matched his lighter moods. But as opposition had worn thin, so too did these new diversions. The hollowness, the emptiness of life once more grew upon him, and his despair flared out. In that mood the casual injustice of a great Power towards an unknown Spaniard became a monstrous violation of human rights upon which he poured all his invective. He knew too well the helpless plight of the wronged and the neglected, not to find an echoing response in his own heart. When he dragged himself to London from Bath or Tunbridge Wells, Pitt began to take, what in a sense was most natural to him, the line of the minority. He had viewed with mounting distrust Newcastle's eagerness to secure alliances with German electors in return for subsidies and he was in no state to keep his distrust to himself. He upbraided Newcastle in private, and marked his disapproval in public by absenting himself from all debates which touched German affairs. His mood from 1751-4 was incalculable and explosive, but in everything he did there was an undertow of despair.

It was partly disease and it was partly disappointment. Since the day Pitt had entered office many reshuffles of the ministry had taken place, but never once had it been suggested that he should be promoted to greater responsibility. Henry Pelham and the Duke of Newcastle valued his advice on both military and foreign affairs; at times they were glad to use his services to patch up their own quarrels. Yet they could see no point in shifting him to higher office, and certainly not when there were the claims of men such as the Duke of Bedford to be considered. Bedford possessed considerable electoral patronage and wide family connections, whereas what little influence the Pitt family possessed was exerted on behalf of the opposition because it was in the hands of Pitt's eccentric brother, Thomas, who had quarrelled with the Stowe House group. And furthermore, Pitt's supporters, the Grenvilles, were in office and collecting honours for themselves. They were happy and thought Pitt well provided for. In the darker moments Pitt must have asked himself if he was to be the perpetual Paymaster. In changing from opposition to office, had he merely exchanged one frustration for another? His temperament suffered a steady disintegration. But for once chance came to his rescue, giving a new thirst, a new excitement, and a need for concentration outside the circle of his own temperament. Henry Pelham died suddenly and Pitt fell in love.

Henry Pelham was not a great statesman, but his qualities have been underestimated because his early career was overshadowed by Sir Robert Walpole and his maturity by Pitt. His views on domestic affairs were sound, liberal, well in advance of his time; about foreign policy he thought very much as Pitt thought, but he was infinitely more circumspect. He had learned all that could be learned from Walpole of the art of handling men, and for ten years he had held together a most heterogeneous collection of politicians in a common purpose. Opposition had ceased almost to exist. But by his death many men saw an opportunity to make a bid for power.

The prospect excited Pitt but he was too ill to leave Bath. Lyttelton was deputed to act as leader of the Stowe House group in all ministerial negotiations. At the same time Pitt carried on an elaborate, guarded correspondence with all the principals. They were mysterious letters, full of the most ornate courtesy, fulsome in their abject submission to the royal pleasure, yet streaked with resentment at long continuance in a minor office. Although there was a constant reiteration of the need to avoid faction and opposition, the threat of it could be read between every line. Nevertheless he failed. The King still hated Pitt and would not have him. Neither Newcastle nor his trusted friend Hardwicke, the Lord Chancellor, were willing to bring on themselves royal displeasure by fighting for him, for his following among men of power was too inconsiderable. In any case Lyttleton betrayed him, allowing himself to be bought off by a dignified place at Court. When Pitt was finally passed over both as Chancellor of the Exchequer and Leader of the House of Commons for a couple of second-rate and incompetent politicians his fury lashed out, but he still stressed his resolution to avoid opposition and gave no indication of an intention to resign. Newcastle and Hardwicke were worried, but they drew a foolish comfort from Pitt's protestations of loyalty and quickly turned their minds from the sense of shame which these words of Pitt must have brought them.

" The weight of irremovable royal displeasure is a load too great to move under: it must crush any man; it has sunk and broke me. I succumb; and wish for nothing but a decent and innocent retreat, wherein I may no longer, by continuing in the public stream of promotion, for ever stick fast aground, and afford the world the ridiculous spectacle of being passed by every boat that navigates the same river."

The early summer of 1754 was one of the darkest moments of Pitt's career. His bid had failed. His wounded pride and his deep sense of great powers denied were forcing him to quit office. He was forty-five years of age, broken in health. Once more he would be near to penury, for his modest private means were insufficient to support the comforts of life to which he had become attached during his years as Pay-master. He had no prospects; none. The warm regard of a small faction, but the implacable hostility of men in power. Riddled with gout, and troubled as he was with the horrors of his despair, a return to a fierce fighting opposition must have seemed impossible. ' A decent and innocent retreat,' a cry from the heart from one battered and injured by fate and his fellow-men.

Then suddenly, as this dark summer turned to autumn, Pitt fell in love. He had known Hester Grenville since his earliest days at Stowe when she was a little girl of nine. For over twenty years he had paid her the attentions courtesy demanded, but nothing more. Love was far from his heart when he rode to Woolton in September, for he was planning to make only a brief stay there. By the beginning of October the marriage settlement was being drawn up and Pitt was bombarding Lady Hester with singular love-letters. Probably he had always had difficulty in expressing himself simply and naturally and certainly by the time he had reached the age of forty-five he had grown accustomed to hiding his sentiments in a mass of verbiage, and ornate phraseology. In consequence many have dismissed his love-letters as hypocritical exercises in fashionable sentimentality, made ridiculous by his age and broken health. Love is not youth's perquisite. In spite of the artificiality of their style, these letters betray a love that was genuine, deep, and life-lasting both for him and for her. There were to be times in his life when neither his wife nor his children could save him from the depths of his melancholy, but what contentment and happiness he achieved was achieved with them. They became his sheet anchor, his tenuous hold on the warm sentient world of ordinary men.

The immediate effect of his marriage was to give him new vigour; to give him the strength he needed to join battle, if need be alone, with the entrenched battalions of Newcastle and Hardwicke. Political society had expected him to drift along unhappily in the wake of the government, snapping at it, but not dangerously; they were startled when in November Pitt turned on the House, upbraiding it for its levity, for its cynicism, for its lack of dignity, and for its connivance at corruption. Horace Walpole watched the faces on the front bench turn pale and he hurried from the Commons to spread the gossip that Pitt, the patriot, was once more stalking the land.

4

The Bid for Power

NEWCASTLE AND HARDWICKE were not unduly alarmed by Pitt's outburst, irritating though it must have been, involved as they were in political negotiations of great delicacy. The death of Henry Pelham had given rise to endless schemes for the construction of a *system*, the word which eighteenth-century politicians used for a ministry. Both Newcastle and Hardwicke would have preferred a more active post for Pitt; they went so far as to sound the King, but his implacable hostility made them drop the idea. It is doubtful whether they expected that their manœuvres would drive Pitt into total opposition. They realised that he would be disappointed, angered even, but no doubt they hoped not beyond the point of management. Although the ornate epistles from Bath had bored them greatly, they had certainly failed to disturb their complacency. In any case, wise politicians that they were, they were more troubled by the problem of Henry Fox than the fate of Pitt. Pitt had no considerable faction, and one of its leading members had secured promotion. Pitt had been happy enough as Paymaster for eight years. He was old, he had no money; he wrote incessantly about the necessity to avoid faction or break the unity of the ministry, words which could be interpreted as face-saving in case he had to remain as Paymaster. To Hardwicke and Newcastle Pitt was an awkward and irritating distraction to a political problem which required all of their *finesse*, the elimination of Henry Fox.

Henry Fox was a gifted friend of the King's favourite son, the Duke of Cumberland. He was married to a daughter of the Duke of Richmond. His connections were as large as his talents were distinguished. The King wanted him. Hardwicke feared and hated him. Newcastle did not care for Fox, but he was too stricken by grief at his brother's death to play much part in the negotiations. How to exclude him from the ministry without infuriating the King, Cumberland, and all of Fox's relations and friends? Hardwicke had been in politics for thirty-five years; an astute apprentice of Sir Robert Walpole's, he had become a master of Cabinet intrigue, and immensely powerful through his long continuance in office as Lord Chancellor. Newcastle was dependent on his skill and strength of character. But this problem of Fox was probably one of the trickiest problems that ever came Hardwicke's way. Its solution has an almost mathematical beauty. Fox was offered the leadership of the House of Commons. He accepted with alacrity and joy, but unastutely made inquiries about conditions *after* and not *before* his acceptance. Then he discovered that he was to have no voice in the disposal of patronage nor even to know who was in receipt of pensions. He was to lead the Commons, but he was to be deprived of the reality of power which lay in the capacity to gratify its members. Fox considered this an intolerable position, said so, and refused the office which he had too eagerly accepted. The King was persuaded that Fox was too difficult to work with, that he had spurned the most generous offers. Both Fox and Pitt had the mortification of seeing places for which they longed filled with men of the meanest capacities; a situation which drew them into sympathetic alliance. But Hardwicke had been too clever by half.

Newcastle quickly realised this and decided that Pitt and Fox would be too formidable if they should act vigorously in opposition. What was he to do— placate one or both? The King was old, over seventy, and might die any year, in which case the Duke of Cumberland would become the most considerable figure at Court, for the heir to the throne was only sixteen. Cumberland was Fox's patron. Having Fox would enable him to become a dominant force which might overwhelm them at the King's death. Yet if the King lived two or three years, his heir would become of age, then regency would no longer be necessary, and the Duke of Cumberland would not acquire power. This situation created an unpleasant dilemma for Newcastle. He was aware, too, that the King's loathing for Pitt could not be changed. Newcastle tried half-heartedly, and with little hope, to secure Pitt as leader of the Commons without an improvement in his status, saying that he would be treated with confidence and always consulted on questions of policy. Pitt was obdurate. So it had to be Fox, who had been in a frenzy of anxiety to get into office, and was now regretting his precipitation in backing out of the former offer in spite of its limitations. Fox was easily won over, and once in the Cabinet forswore all connection with Pitt, an act of treachery which Pitt never forgave.

Henry Pelham had died in March, 1754, yet after twelve months of negotiation the ministry was still unsettled. Letters, conferences, flashes of opposition and prolonged bouts of abstention from debates had all been used by Pitt without any success. Even the most prolonged diplomacy must have an end either in compromise or war. Throughout this time Pitt had remained as Paymaster-General and he had been allowed to remain so quite deliberately by Newcastle, who hoped that bursts of opposition might subside or that some arrangement could be made with him. In the summer of 1755 the stakes grew higher. Pitt was known to be in consultation at Leicester House, the home of the Dowager Princess of Wales, who loathed the Duke of Cumberland, hated Fox and bore no love for Newcastle. This was the broadest hint Pitt had yet made that unless his demands were met outright opposition would follow. Once more Hardwicke sounded Pitt, but he came away deeply troubled. Pitt demanded not only a secretaryship of state and leadership of the Commons, but also a change of policy. In the event of a European war, Hanover was to be left to its fate, to be recompensed at the peace for any tribulations which it might have suffered. This policy would permit a cut in German subsidies upon which Pitt insisted. These were extravagantly high terms. But Pitt's mood was lofty. The humiliations of years were not to be easily wiped out. And maybe he did not wish his terms to be accepted. Opposition offered much for which Pitt's nature craved—release from frustration, unbridled emotion, public fame.

The break came when, during the parliamentary sessions in November, Pitt made one of the very greatest speeches of his life. He denounced the German subsidy treaties which the government, fearing war, had recently signed.

" Are these treaties English measures? Are they preventative measures, as has been said in debate? Are they not measures of aggression? . . . If a war in Europe ensues from these negotiations I will always follow up the authors of this measure. They must mean a land-war and how preposterously do they mediate it. Hanover is the only spot you have left to fight upon. . . . But my objection to the choice of Hanover as our battle ground is not from fear of prejudices but from its locality; for, alas! we cannot suspend the laws of nature and make Hanover not an open defenceless country. . . . But the strangest argument in these treaties is that, if our navies are defeated, we can turn our eyes to these mercenaries as a reserve. . . . If you must go and traffic with the Czarina for succour, why, rather than her troops, did not you hire twenty ships? I will say why—because ships could not be applied to Hanover. . . . I do not know what majorities will do, but this I do know, that these treaties will hang like a millstone about the neck of any minister, and sink him along with the nation."

This speech of Pitt's was not only important because it made his dismissal certain but also because it was his first clear exposition of how he considered a war should be fought. An alliance should be made with Frederick of Prussia, the only Power in Europe capable of containing France. Any other continental system would be both expensive and useless. England's power should be used on her natural element—the sea: the aim—to defeat France overseas, particularly in America, where our colonists, those ' long-injured, long-neglected, long-forgotten people,' were in danger of being overwhelmed by the French. It was a clear call to sacrifice Hanover and pursue British interests. The King's anger with Pitt grew more intense, but the City was relieved to hear its aspirations voiced so unequivocally.

After this speech Pitt was dismissed from office. He was saved from penury by his brother-in-law, Earl Temple, who gave him an annuity of £1000 p.a., a fact which Pitt publicised wherever he went. It underlined his heroic sacrifices and Pitt never welcomed a secret martyrdom. Also he needed all the publicity he could muster in order to secure such a clamour against the ministry that both George II and Newcastle would be forced to accept his terms.

At first events did not favour him. For many months

war had threatened. Sporadic fighting between the French and the English in America and India had never ceased since the war of the Austrian Succession. France had steadily built up her fleets and armies for a renewed contest. The reinforcement of her forces in Canada had been one of her objects and to circumvent this a fleet under Admiral Boscawen had been sent to intercept the French ships off the coast of Canada. In this Boscawen was partially successful and his capture of two vessels was vaunted in the government press. A greater stroke of luck followed. Frederick of Prussia learned of the secret understanding between Austria and France; these old enemies, now reconciled, threatened to destroy him in isolation. Added to this was the implied threat to Prussia in the recent treaty between Russia and Great Britain. Frederick expressed his willingness to guarantee the neutrality of Hanover in case of war. The ministry swallowed the proffered bait at once. The Convention of Westminster was signed. The fact that Britain now had treaty obligations with both Frederick and one of his main enemies, Russia, caused no misgivings. Hanover was under the protection of the strongest army in Europe. In the light of that fact, any other obligations were insignificant. Furthermore, the sting of one of Pitt's main criticisms was drawn. For years he had harped on the necessity of a Prussian alliance. He was silenced on that score.

Events did not continue long to run Newcastle's way. Disaster piled on disaster. In America, General Braddock was defeated and killed; our attacks on

French Canada frustrated. Fully mobilised France was poised to strike. Her army in the Pas de Calais was prepared to invade England; diversionary attacks were planned on Ireland and Scotland, Nova Scotia and Minorca—our great Mediterranean base. The memory of the ''45' was still green and the threat of invasion scared the country. Everyone knew that our troops were too few: a plan for a new militia, strongly backed by Pitt, had recently been rejected by the House of Lords. Panic and dissatisfaction with the government began to spread. The French judged— perhaps rightly—that a direct invasion across the Channel was too bold a gamble. Rapidly switching his forces, Marshal Belleisle attacked Minorca in strength. The Mediterranean squadron under Admiral Byng fought an indecisive action with a superior French fleet and retired to Gibraltar. Deprived of naval support the Minorcan garrison quickly surrendered.

Rage and fear consumed the country. The City of London exercised its immemorial right to address the King. Condign punishment for those responsible for our defeat was demanded in outspoken terms, and a change of policy strongly pressed; the City prayed " that the large supplies so necessarily called for, and so cheerfully granted, may be religiously applied to the defence of these Kingdoms and colonies and their commerce." The common people expressed themselves more bluntly. A terrified Newcastle heard them going about the streets chanting " Hang Byng or take care of your King." Newcastle was all for hanging Byng as quickly as possible if it would appease the country.

At the same time he fretfully pleaded for immediate action—Mediterranean, America, West Indies—anywhere so long as it obliterated the disgrace of Minorca. But action came from the French. At Fort Oswego, on Lake Ontario, British forces were annihilated.

" Minorca is gone, Oswego gone," Horace Walpole wailed. " The nation is in a ferment. Instructions from counties, boroughs, especially the City of London, in the style of 1641 . . . all these tell Pitt he may command such numbers without doors as may make majorities within the House tremble."

The trial of Byng was insufficient to delude the nation. Henry Fox was astute enough to realise that the public situation was so grave that a ministerial crisis of gravity could be provoked with the chance that Newcastle and Hardwicke might be overthrown; if so, he and Pitt might share supreme power. He risked the gamble and made high demands on Newcastle and backed them with a threat of resignation. Newcastle sank under the weight of responsibilities which were too grave for his ineffective and anxious temperament. Nor did the granite obduracy of Hardwicke avail them. Slowly and patiently he tried every move, every trick that years of political experience had taught him. Pitt without Fox; Fox without Pitt; Pitt and Fox: at last he saw there was no hope. He indicated his intention to retire from politics, an acknowledgment of his defeat.

It was Pitt and not Fox who won. The old, tired obstinate King was hard pressed, yet even his mistress, Lady Yarmouth, insisted that Pitt must have power.

Grudgingly the King gave way, but Pitt was not prepared to be gracious. He made his conditions crystal
clear; they were these: he would not serve with
Newcastle, an inquiry into past measures must be
undertaken, an immediate Militia Bill must be passed,
and finally he himself was to have direct access to the
King and be responsible for the formulation of policy
—tough terms, utterly disagreeable to the King. Pitt
developed gout and remained at his country house.
Days of intrigue and argument followed until in the
end Pitt, backed by the Stowe House clan, won
through. The King was obstinate on one point. He
would not permit Pitt to be Secretary of State for the
Northern Provinces, which was considered the more
important of the two Secretaryships of State, because
it included Hanover.

Wise politicians did not view the new ministry with
any confidence. The Stowe House faction, although
powerful, was small and lacked sufficient subordinates
to fill the minor offices; men who had been loyal for
years to Hardwicke and Newcastle had to be kept in
their places, an ever-present danger to Pitt's security.
And Horace Walpole, who had much of his father's
political wisdom, if none of his ability, wrote :

" Mr. Pitt accedes with so little strength that his
success seems very precarious. If he Hanoverizes, or
checks any inquiries, he loses his popularity, and
falls that way; if he humours the rage of the people
he provokes two powerful factions.[1] His only chance

[1] i.e. Newcastle's and Fox's.

seems to depend on joining with the Duke of Newcastle who is most offended with Fox: but after
Pitt's personal exclusion of his Grace, and considering
Pitt's small force, it may not be easy for him to be
accepted there. I foresee nothing but confusion: the
new system is composed of such discordant parts
that it can produce no harmony."

Events justified this analysis. Treacherous men in the
Cabinet, a reluctant King, colleagues such as Temple
who became overbearingly proud and arrogant, all of
these factors distracted Pitt and prevented his ministry
from exercising the authority needed to wage a war of
imperial magnitude. Within four months everything
was high confusion. The Duke of Cumberland,
appointed as Commander-in-Chief of allied forces in
Hanover, flatly refused to receive orders from a
government containing Pitt, words which were sweet
and welcome to the King. Out went Pitt, and the
Cousinhood followed. But it was easier to break
ministries than to create them. Days of farce followed.
On one occasion, Fox, Robinson and others were
dressed in their finest, confidently awaiting the royal
call to accept the seals which Newcastle had negotiated
for them. They waited in vain. A letter from Lord
Chesterfield, maintaining that no ministry could survive
without Pitt, so flurried the Duke that he tore up his
arrangements and began again. Meanwhile city after
city conferred its freedom on Pitt in boxes of gold.
There could only be one end. Government there must
be. Pitt without Newcastle and Newcastle without

Pitt could not provide it. Coalition was forced on them. The division of powers was clear and simple. Newcastle was to find the money and control the Commons; Pitt manage the war. Once decided a ministry was easily constructed. Old Hardwicke, who, since Henry Pelham's death, had been in charge of the negotiations, spent three happy days in the nice distribution of places to relatives, friends, and hangers-on. He was scrupulously fair; there were fat pickings for the Cousinhood, nor did he forget Pitt's school friends, nor his own son-in-law. It was neat, tidy and deeply gratifying. The chaos created by Henry Pelham's death was at last resolved.

At forty-nine Pitt achieved supreme power. He was on the threshold of greatness and immortality. Yet the years had taken their toll. He was a more remote, more intricate personality, and his poses, artificialities, and exaggerations had strengthened with use. The flame that was within him did not always shine out with brilliance, too frequently it was obscured, for he had been forced to adapt himself to the intimate politics of his time for which he had no gifts.

This had been Pitt's dilemma. In opposition the world was his. He could rally London and the great merchant towns to his banner. His attitude was their attitude; his voice, their voice. But that availed little. Walpole had demonstrated time and time again that public clamour could be ignored, one of his many lessons that the Pelhams and the King had learnt. As a patriot, Pitt could frighten and scare governments; he could make ministers feel that he must be placated.

All this was possible for him and frequently accomplished. But at that point his weakness was laid bare. He lacked the followers to fill a ministry. His connection was noisy, arrogant, and not without ability, but it was pitifully small. Pitt knew it as everyone knew it. So he felt it necessary to play the game of politics on Newcastle's and Hardwicke's terms. The patriot would disappear, and the politician emerge—reasonable, accommodating, reluctant to offend. These were the bewildering faceabout turns which destroyed his popularity overnight and brought his sincerity under suspicion.

Of his ultimate sincerity there can be no question. He hated the Bourbons, and longed passionately for the realisation of his dream of Empire. That was why it was so easy for him to recreate the popularity which he momentarily lost. No one could mistake his genuine convictions, nor his sense of mission. But he needed power, and in the world of politics in which he found himself Pitt was lost. He made the wrong offers at the wrong times, threatened when threats carried no weight, complied too easily and too late. In spite of the brilliance of his intellectual gifts he was always out-manœuvred by dull-witted men. Events alone saved Pitt from shipwreck. As his country crashed from disaster to disaster, men were glad to surrender the reins of power into his eager and willing hands. " I know that I can save the country and that I alone can." Lofty words of a mad arrogance at which many sneered and others tittered. Time proved them.

* 5 *

The Triumph

The City of London, as long as they have any memory, cannot forget that you accepted the seals when this nation was in the most deplorable circumstances to which any country can be reduced, our trade exposed to the enemy, our credit, as if we expected to become bankrupt, sunk to the worst pitch; that there was nothing to be found but despondency at home and contempt abroad. The City must also for ever remember that when you resigned the seals, our armies and navies were victorious, our trade secure and flourishing more than in peace, our public credit restored, and people readier to lend than ministers to borrow.

IN FIVE years Pitt implanted an indelible memory into the mind of the nation, a memory which for two centuries has helped sustain it in tribulation and danger of defeat. In these years the foundations of imperial greatness were laid which survived both the loss of America and the onslaught of Napoleon, only to be eroded by the slow process of time.

When he accepted office in 1756 Pitt needed the elevation of spirit which suffused him. Prostrate with gout, he summoned his secretaries to his bedside at Hayes and remodelled the instructions to commanders and their plans of campaign, a reorganisation which the short intermission of office did little to delay. But although Pitt worked with phrenetic energy he could not stem the tide of disaster. The loss of Minorca had been but the beginning. Byng was shot in spite of the protests of Pitt who courted unpopularity for the sake of justice. He knew that the ministry was as much to blame as Byng, and furthermore that the safety of his fleet had been of paramount importance when the depleted condition of the navy was considered. Defeats in America and India followed; our colonies and our trade were at the mercy of France.

This was Pitt's inheritance. For years the situation of our colonists had deteriorated in America. Towards the end of the seventeenth century the French fur trappers in their search for beaver had begun to move out from the Great Lakes towards the headwaters of the Mississippi. This great river, once discovered, drew them down towards the Gulf of Mexico, where in the early part of the eighteenth century New Orleans and Louisiana flourished. A chain of forts was built to protect French traders. The English colonists in America realised with dismay that they were in danger of being cut off from the rich fur territories, west of the Alleghenies, and confined to the coast. It was not only the growing French monopoly of the fur trade which alarmed the colonists. The hardy fishermen of New England were in constant conflict with the Breton sailors in the great cod fishing ground at the Grand Banks of Newfoundland. Here, too, the American and English fishermen learned to grow jealous of the French. And to thoughtful men both in America and England, these fishing grounds had a greater importance than their fish. They were the breeding grounds of sailors, whose hardy lives fitted them for the brutality of war. For years Pitt's friends in America and in London had warned him of the growing French power and explained its danger both to our commerce and our power at sea. And the French in Canada had this further advantage. They were organised on a military basis; action could follow rapidly from decision. By contrast the English plantations were controlled by their own argumentative legislatures, frequently more interested in local jealousies than the conflict of nations.

In India the situation was little better. In the days of Governor Pitt there were very few Englishmen living in India and they were confined to small trading posts or factories at Madras, Calcutta, Surat and Bombay. Relations with the Indians varied greatly. Some traders adopted Indian habits of life, learnt the language and married Indian women; others, like Governor Pitt, had a low opinion of the natives; considering their government utterly corrupt and their merchants dishonest. Nevertheless no one thought that the relationship between Englishmen and Hindus should be anything but mercantile. There was no question of subjecting India to British power. Such a policy would have struck Governor Pitt as an impossibility, and inimical to British interests. This attitude was transformed in the middle years of the eighteenth century by the chaotic political conditions which followed the death of the last great Mogul Emperor,

Aurangzeb. Even he had failed to maintain the fiction of unity. The wandering Maratha princes had resisted all attempts to crush them. But as soon as Aurangzeb was dead, they terrorised North and Central India, flouting successfully the authority of the titular Emperor at Delhi. This encouraged Imperial governors elsewhere to adopt an attitude of independence. By 1740 the great Mogul Empire lay in ruins, presenting a vast opportunity for plunder to the soldier-adventurer.

The French were the first to realise what could be won. In Dupleix they possessed a general of originality and daring. He trained native troops in Western methods and put them under the command of French officers. In action he trusted in gunpowder and boldness of decision. Both were effective. By 1749 he was in complete control of Madras. His success intoxicated him and he dreamed of a French empire stretching across Central India, an empire in which no Englishman traded. But his actions betrayed his dreams and the English East India Company planned bitter resistance. Recklessly, Dupleix divided his forces and gave the British their chance. His boldness was outmatched by Robert Clive, who achieved instant immortality by his defeat of the French at Arcot (1751).

Temperamentally Clive and Pitt had much in common. Clive, too, was haunted by a despair so dark that he attempted suicide: in the end he died by his own hand. He found an anodyne in acute physical danger. Impossible odds were an exaltation and in the very jaws of death he discovered life's purpose and its satisfaction. He relished the defeat of his enemies. He treated them with brutal arrogance, extracting from them fabulous concessions for the Company and extravagant wealth for himself. He combined the temperament of a suicide with the appetite of a pirate. His success stirred the French to greater efforts. Both Dupleix and Clive had made it clear how easy it was to win power in India and how great was the booty. Neither country was prepared to share or to compromise.

The struggle between France and Britain was not confined to India and America. In the West Indies the great sugar islands of Guadeloupe and Martinique were a threat to British monopoly. On the African coast they fought for slaves, ivory and gold. Wherever men traded, from Archangel to the China Seas, the rivalry of France and Britain deepened and festered. In 1756, when war broke out in Europe, the trade of the world was at stake.

The odds were heavily against England. The population of France was more than double that of England. Through the long years of peace after Utrecht (1713) France had steadily increased her naval power. Her army was admitted to be one of the most efficient in Europe. This was in marked contrast with the conditions which faced Pitt when he assumed power. Many officers regarded the regiments which they had bought as fit objects of plunder; dead men and deserters were kept on the books for the sake of their pay. Contractors made exorbitant profits for the provision of deplorable materials. The hardship

Plate 3.   *The Earl of Hardwicke, by Thomas Hudson*

Plate 4. Caricature of Chatham in the House of Commons

and brutality of the service made enlistment difficult. The same inefficiency, the same corruption, was rife in the navy; many of our ships were so foul that they were unable to remain long at sea. A small ill-equipped army and a navy which was rotting through inaction and maladministration were the tools which Pitt found to hand. And at the moment of his accession to power, the French were poised to strike. In Canada they had pushed their outposts down the Hudson and Mohawk rivers to threaten New York; a further concentration at Fort Duquesne menaced Baltimore and Virginia. In India, the princes were determined to throw off the heavy yoke of Clive and destroy British power. In Europe France had consolidated her alliances with Austria and Russia; and Frederick the Great ringed round with enemies seemed doomed to a rapid destruction.

And yet Pitt had no doubts that he could save the country and win the war. He had already decided on his measures. They were these: The army was to be freed by raising a county militia for the protection of the country from French invasion, and it was to be strengthened by raising two Highland regiments, thereby making use of the best natural soldiers in Britain, and, by so doing, lessening the danger of Scots discontent and Jacobite rebellion. This army was to be used for a series of attacks on the French coast which Pitt thought would lead the French to concentrate large forces at home and so weaken their attack on Frederick. Frederick was to be more directly aided by subsidies and by the provision of an army of

C.   E observation in Hanover, designed to protect his flank from the French. The aim of this policy was to make the maximum use of small forces, a policy with which Frederick himself was in agreement. The only further demand which he made was for action of a similar nature in both the Baltic and the Mediterranean.

The major attack was to be made on French colonies and their commerce. To accomplish this it was essential that England should maintain her supremacy at sea. It became vital to prevent a concentration of the French Atlantic and Mediterranean fleets, and in order to do so Pitt instituted a system of close blockade of the chief French naval bases—Brest, Rochefort, and Toulon. And there was this further danger. Spain was sympathetic to French ambitions and Spain possessed a fine navy. If they allied, England would be at a grave disadvantage. It was this contingency which, in the early years of the war, gave rise to the astonishing spectacle of Pitt using all his arts and blandishments to secure the neutrality of Spain.

France, contained in Europe, was to be destroyed overseas. The strategy of his colonial attack had long been worked out in consultation with his merchant friends. Louisburg and Quebec were the keys to Canada. French influence in West Africa would be destroyed by taking Goree. The capture of Guadeloupe and Martinique would secure the West Indies. In India, Pitt was prepared to leave the struggle to Clive whom he described as a ' heaven born general,' confining his help to naval protection and the destruction of France's advanced naval base at Mauritius.

The beauty of this policy lay in the fact that every activity was intimately related and all designed to serve a common purpose, not only the defeat of France, but also to wrest from her the commerce of the world. Such a policy bred fear, and fear bred critics. The memory of Marlborough was not dead. His victories had been won on the battlefields of Europe, through close military co-operation with our European allies. By such action he had brought France to the verge of total ruin. Furthermore, some of Pitt's tactics had been tried before. Attacks had been twice mounted against Louisburg and Quebec, but these attempts to dislodge the French from Canada had ended in failure. And some argued there might be a subtle danger even in victory. France would never sign a treaty which stripped her of her colonies and trade; or, if she did, it would merely be a truce to reserve her energies for a renewed struggle. Nor would Europe quietly watch the realisation of such vaunting ambition. England would raise up against herself a formidable coalition of powers. Such a policy as Pitt's might lead as easily to the ruin and desolation of Britain as the humiliation of France. Criticisms such as these were frequently heard wherever men met to discuss the plight of their country. At first they were stilled by peril, and then for a time forgotten in the intoxication of Pitt's victories, only to emerge with renewed force, when the fulfilment of Pitt's dreams was at hand.

The first speech which Pitt drafted for the King made his purpose quite clear. " The success and preservation of America cannot but constitute a main object of my attention and solicitude, and the growing dangers to which our colonies stand exposed from our late losses in those parts, demand resolution of vigour and despatch." But the implementation was difficult to carry out. The ships of the navy were in a bad condition and continuous blockade of French ports could not be maintained; French reinforcements slipped out from the Atlantic ports to Canada and the West Indies.

In India Bengal was in turmoil; Calcutta had been lost and its British inhabitants massacred in the Black Hole. The first combined operation against the French coast, at Rochefort, ended in fiasco, for the commanding officers decided to withdraw without attacking; an example which was followed in America when an attempt on Louisburg was abandoned without a shot being fired. But the worst news came from Germany. The Duke of Cumberland's army of observation was crushed by the French at the Battle of Hastenbeck. With the connivance of the King, and without consulting Frederick of Prussia, Cumberland made peace with the French. Pitt declared that this action was made solely by George II as Elector of Hanover and could never be ratified by England. Small comfort for Frederick, engulfed on all sides by enemies more powerful than himself. Feeble and ineffective action, coupled with defeat, bred despair.

The prevailing gloom was heightened by domestic unrest. The harvests had failed, and disturbances were widespread. The situation was made worse by what appeared to be duplicity in the operation of the

Militia Act. Volunteers in Huntingdonshire had been shipped off for service overseas, an act which smacked of sharp practice. The popularity both of the militia and of the government was further diminished by rumours of peculation and graft. The first months of Pitt's renewed ministry were darkened by defeat abroad and despondency at home. Horace Walpole wrote gloomily that ' it is time for England to slip her own cables and float away into some unknown sea.'

Those timid of heart thought peace, and a peace without honour, would not long be delayed. Pitt was preoccupied, aloof and furiously busy, and much more interested in the spate of intelligence reports which were pouring in to his office than in the fears and timidities of his colleagues.

News from India gave the first indication that the tide might be turning. The Black Hole of Calcutta had stirred Clive to decisive action. In conjunction with Admiral Watson he made a rapid counter-attack on the French at Fort William (Calcutta) and Chandernagore. They were quickly overwhelmed and without pause, Clive turned inland to deal with the great native army of Suraja Dowlah which controlled the provinces of Bengal, Bihar and Orissa. The two armies met at Plassey on June 23rd 1757. Suraja Dowlah had sixty thousand native troops at his disposal; Clive nine hundred white troops and about two thousand, English trained, natives. Rarely have numbers been so unequal in battle. But Clive relished the odds. By effective use of fire-power and superb daring, he scattered Dowlah's army. The victory was immense, for Clive had not only defeated an army but secured possession of three of the richest provinces in India; in a day he had changed the future of a continent.

This relieved Pitt of a great burden for he decided that India could well be left to Clive and the Company. He was prepared to send a naval squadron to give support and to attack Mauritius which he regarded as the strategic base of French naval strength in the Indian Ocean. He was not prepared to do much more. Later Clive was to offer to acquire the sovereignty of the three great provinces which he had conquered:

> " I flatter myself I have made it pretty clear to you," he wrote to Pitt, " that there will be little or no difficulty in obtaining the absolute possession of these rich Kingdoms . . . Now I leave you to judge whether an income yearly of upwards of two millions sterling, with the possession of three provinces abounding in the most valuable productions of nature and art, be an object deserving the public attention."

Pitt refused the bait. He was not interested in the subjection of alien races to an imperial rule. Such a development in India was to disturb him profoundly. To cripple French trade in India was his sole aim. He desired nothing more. Hence, for Pitt, the acquisition of Mauritius was more important than the subjection of Bengal, but unfortunately less easy to achieve. Clive was determined to rule Bengal, and if the government refused, then the Company must. And the Company did. When at last Pitt was able to mount an attack against Mauritius in January, 1761, it failed. Unable to ' lay the axe to the root ' of French power, it was only a generation before they became once more formidable in India. But, even so, India required little of his concentration, for he had deep confidence in Clive's military powers, even though he suspected his political judgment.

Canada and the West Indies required greater attention, and they were the preoccupation of his closest city friends—Beckford, Vaughan, Sawbridge and Janssen. Pitt was fully informed of the topography and its strategic and tactical possibilities. He had received careful evaluations of colonial strength and of the reliability of Indian allies. Army commanders and private individuals had urged on him their favourite schemes. All was ready; all was assimilated. Carefully, Pitt laid his plans for the great conquest of Canada.

There were grave difficulties. Communications with commanders in Canada were, of necessity, very slow; instructions might be months crossing the Atlantic before reaching their destination. Co-operation with colonial troops was extremely difficult for each of the thirteen colonies raised its own forces. These troops were below British standards in equipment and in discipline, and they were only enlisted for short periods. Further, the colonists hated the redcoats almost as much as they hated the French. Nor was this all. Seniority in the British army was most strictly adhered to. Pitt knew well enough that the Canadian war required young men of bold spirit. But the King insisted on the direction of the campaigns remaining in the hands of his senior officers. And again, Canada called for combined operations, for the close co-operation between the army and navy, yet they had rarely worked together, and both officers and men were suspicious and jealous of each other. In these circumstances Pitt could not have been

The Conquest of Canada

blamed had he set himself limited objectives. But to do so was alien to his nature; his schemes for Canada were grandiose. They ignored difficulty and challenged fate.

From the point of view of strategy the conquest of Canada was simple. It could be attacked from the south, using New York as a base and the Hudson river and its great lakes of Champlain and George as lines of communication, for rivers were all important in a country which lacked roads. The St. Lawrence offered an equally effective entry for forces based on Halifax. Naturally the French were thoroughly aware of the strategic implications of these routes and they had built forts at Louisburg and Ticonderoga to act as bastions of defence or springboards for attack. A similar bastion, Fort Duquesne, protected the communications of the French in Canada with those in the South and at the same time threatened British communications between Virginia and New England. On 30 October 1757 Pitt sent out his plan of attack. Abercromby with a mixed British and colonial force was to sweep up the Hudson valley to Montreal, and if opportunity allowed to Quebec. A combined force, the army under Amherst and the navy led by Boscawen, were to reduce Louisburg, sail up the St. Lawrence and assault Quebec. Forbes, one of the few British generals admired by the colonists, was to capture Fort Duquesne in alliance with friendly Indian tribes.

At last piecemeal tactics were laid aside and the French in Canada subjected to a powerful concentric attack. The difficulties of co-ordination were immense; the movements of armies and navies painfully slow; the negotiations with hostile Indian tribes protracted. By the time the campaign was launched, half the summer was gone.

Abercromby's stately progress up the Hudson, gave Montcalm, the greatest of the French generals, ample

time to create a barrier of great defensive strength at
Ticonderoga. Abercromby was too good a text-book
general to risk his army in a stroke of bold resolution.
He recognised the check and withdrew. Amherst had
greater success. The daring of the navy and the valour
of the troops under Brigadier Wolfe had effected a
landing near Louisburg in spite of a raging storm and
accurate French fire. But Wolfe was forced to watch
Amherst fritter his advantage away.

"This place," he wrote angrily, "is in an evil
state. It cannot stand a siege. If it had been attacked
by anybody but the English it would have fallen long
ago."

Yet to a siege it was subjected, for Amherst had been
trained in Germany where fortresses were invested,
then mined, battered, and starved into subjection. He
believed in the rules of the game he played and he
kept to them. In due time, on the 26th July 1758
Louisburg surrendered. It was a great victory. The
gateway of the St. Lawrence was ours; Canada was
cut off from its homeland and the possibility of its
reinforcement grew remote. Unhappily the victory,
as the impatient Wolfe saw, could not be exploited;
furthermore, the news of Abercromby's withdrawal
commanded caution. Louisburg was not the sole
success. Forbes had welded together a mixed force of
Indians and colonists. Lightly armed, quick moving,
in a single bold stroke they had destroyed the French
at Fort Duquesne. Proudly Forbes renamed it—
Pittsburg—and ill beyond hope of recovery, returned
to Philadelphia to die.

By the capture of Fort Duquesne and Louisburg Canada was contained, and during the winter of 1758 Pitt laid his plans for the kill. They were an elaboration of the basic strategic scheme. Amherst replaced Abercromby and he was encouraged to make a twofold attack on Canada from the south—one by Ticonderoga to Montreal, the other by the Mohawk river to the Great Lakes where the objective was Fort Niagara. From the St. Lawrence a direct assault was to be made on Quebec and for this operation Pitt secured the command for Wolfe, but not without a great struggle with the King who preferred command of armies to proceed according to due order of seniority, irrespective of military genius—each and every general was to be given his opportunity to fail. But Wolfe had impressed Pitt as he had already impressed both his men and his fellow officers. His letters betrayed his restless, impetuous spirit; the hectic courage of a man who walked constantly with death, for Wolfe was being consumed by tuberculosis. He wanted victory and glory before the sands ran out. Reckless Wolfe might be, but like all great men of action he paid a thorough attention to detail. His men were trained with great care, discipline never relaxed; food, stores, ammunition, never neglected. As in Clive, so in Wolfe, Pitt recognised his spiritual brother; a man like himself who found forgetfulness of self in the elation of action.

Wolfe set about his task with serious expedition. The navy demonstrated its rare skill in negotiating the treacherous waters of the St. Lawrence with its rapid tides and uncharted shoals.[1] Halifax and Louisburg were emptied of troops and left quite defenceless; Wolfe put his trust in the home fleet's blockade of the French Atlantic coast, which he hoped would contain the French forces. Slowly the great flotilla of troop-ships wended its way up the river, but Wolfe was denied the advantage of surprise. Montcalm had intercepted British letters, and realising the danger to Quebec he had withdrawn his troops from Montreal in time to organise its defences. When Wolfe disem-barked his troops on the flats near Quebec, he lacked all advantages of terrain for Montcalm occupied the great heights upon which the citadel was built. He refused to be drawn by Wolfe's harrying tactics on the surrounding settlements. The summer days passed, and victory seemed no nearer. Wolfe was prostrate with his disease, and his days were darkened by the open contempt shown him by his brigadiers. There must have been times when he thought that his life would end in disaster and disgrace. In a moment of despair he asked his officers to draw up their plans to finish a campaign which he was too sick to conduct. Then suddenly life returned to him, a moment of health, a resurgence of energy. Throwing aside the plans which had been submitted to him, he decided to risk all on a gambler's throw. A feint naval demon-stration distracted Montcalm whilst Wolfe ferried during the darkness of night nearly five thousand men across the perilous river to a tiny cove at the foot of

[1] James Cook, the explorer of the Pacific, was one of the master mariners.

the towering Heights of Abraham. By dawn this army was drawn up in battle array on the plateau above, facing the astonished and outnumbered French. Montcalm, fully aware of his danger, attacked at once and with fury, only to see his men slaughtered by the steady, well-disciplined fire of the British. For Wolfe it was victory, immortality, and death.

Elsewhere plans had once more gone awry. Amherst had moved carefully up the Hudson Valley, finding Ticonderoga and Crown Point abandoned. A subsidiary force under Prideaux had cleared the Mohawk Valley and captured Fort Niagara, which brought the Great Lakes under British control. Nevertheless, Montreal remained in French hands with the core of the French army unbeaten. Indeed, the British only just escaped disaster. Copying Wolfe's tactics, scaling, just as he had scaled the Heights of Abraham, the French caught the British unawares in Quebec, but defeat was narrowly averted and the army hung on until it was relieved by the navy forcing its way through the melting ice of the St. Lawrence. This failure to retake Quebec sealed the fate of the French in Canada. Inexorably the British armies converged on Montreal A—mherst from the Great Lakes, Haviland from Ticonderoga, Murray from Quebec. On the 8th September 1760 the French Governor General surrendered Canada. It was a momentous day, for the shattered power of France opened the vast prairies of the West and made it certain that America would be united, thereby avoiding the destiny of a torn and distracted Europe.

A great victory, yet but one of many that Pitt had harvested in these turbulent years. His strategy encompassed the world, and hand in hand with the conquest of Canada had come triumphs in Africa and the West Indies, which were linked in a common destiny by the traffic of slaves. As valuable as the slave trade was the trade in gum of which the French at Goree had obtained a monopoly. This, the ' gum arabick,' was used in the manufacture of the luxurious French fabrics which dominated the fashions of Europe, fabrics which English manufacturers were learning to imitate if not to improve. In Canada, fish and fur; in Africa, gum and slaves, commerce entwined in war, the grand theme of Chatham's strategy.

His forces encountered little serious opposition in West Africa. In 1758 Fort Louis on the Senegal river was captured with booty worth nearly a quarter of a million pounds; later in the year the short campaign was concluded by the capture of Goree (Dakkar), which deprived the French privateers of its fine natural harbour. British merchants followed in the wake of her navies and by the end of the war African trade had flourished so exceedingly that the expedition had more than paid for itself in the increased customs duties. The capture of West Africa was a serious blow to the French in the West Indies, for they were denied the source of their labour and the price of slaves became prohibitive.

But the lack of slaves was to prove the least of the French sugar planters' troubles. On taking office in 1757 Pitt had sketched a scheme of conquest of the

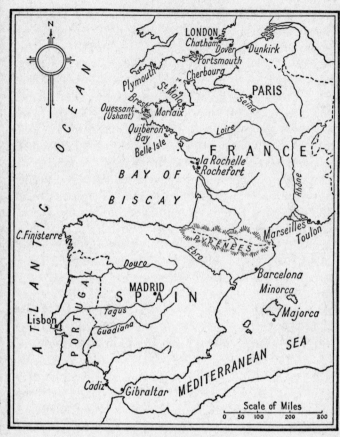

The War at Sea

rich islands of Martinique and Guadeloupe. Both
Hardwicke and Newcastle were disturbed by what
they heard. Both islands were strongly fortified;

both islands expected attack. Their doubts of the wisdom of Pitt's scheme were shared on this occasion by some of Pitt's city friends, notably Beckford, who feared that their capture might lead to a glut of sugar on the London market, followed by a fall in price. Pitt listened with more attention to the pleas of the West Indian colonists who were losing the American market to the French and whose ships were being destroyed by the French privateers. At the first attempt, Martinique proved too strong for the British forces under General Hopson, who had to content himself with the taking of Guadeloupe, the capital value of which was reckoned at nine and a half million pounds. Under the energetic administration of Governor Crump the output of the islands was doubled within two years. Once more an expedition proved itself to be a rich investment. Yet such were the demands for men and ships in other theatres of war that the final assault was delayed until 1762 when Martinique was captured by Rodney. During the short time it was held by the British it proved as rich a gold mine as Guadeloupe.

The victories which Pitt had won overseas were due to the inability of the French to reinforce their colonial forces and to the fact that their navy was confined to its home ports. The blockade of the French coast in order to prevent the juncture of the Atlantic and Mediterranean fleets of France was throughout the eighteenth century a cardinal point of British naval strategy. Once united, these fleets would threaten our supremacy in the Channel which, if lost, would

Plate 5.   George III, by Thomas Gainsborough

Plate 6. William Pitt, Earl of Chatham. Moulded in wax by an American, Mrs. Patience Wright, and finished in November, 1775

permit invasion, and no one believed the raw, ill-disciplined militia would be a match for the armies of France. Hence, an immense burden rested on our blockading fleets. In all weathers they had to maintain a ceaseless watch on the great French ports of Toulon and Brest. In the early days of the war our ships were too ill-founded to keep a close and continuous blockade, and too frequently they were forced from their stations by the need to refit, which enabled the French to slip reinforcements across to Canada and the West Indies.

But Pitt was ruthlessly energetic and he gave the same detailed attention to naval materials and supplies that he expended on the army, and by the end of the war the navy had reached a pitch of perfection not again equalled until the days of Nelson. Effective blockade enabled Pitt to plan thrusts against the French coast—at St. Malo, Cherbourg and elsewhere. They destroyed valuable war potential and worried the French sufficiently to keep a sizeable army in the West, which gave some relief to Frederick the Great who was handling his superb army with astonishing skill. Outnumbered as he was by his formidable enemies— France, Russia and Austria—yet he kept them at bay by lightning moves and miraculous victories. But he needed men. Reluctant as he was to use our armies on the Continent, Pitt could not deny Frederick completely without risking his defeat. And the country was denuded of men to give him support. England was so barren of troops that her defence was left entirely to the militia which, as the news of Pitt's victories

C. F

came rolling in, achieved great popularity, breeding a martial ardour and enthusiasm for war.

Pitt's victories, it is true, were built on a profound attention to detail without which armies and navies cannot win, no matter how inspired; yet in 1759, the *annus mirabilis*, there was an undeniable *élan*, a will to victory, that was prepared to challenge fate. Wolfe at Quebec was matched by Hawke at Quiberon Bay, where, in the teeth of a gale, he sailed his ships through the rocks and shoals to blast the Brest fleet out of the water, a manœuvre which had the reckless competence of a Nelson. At Minden, too, the army and its officers covered themselves with glory, withstanding the repeated battering of the French cavalry, turning a threatened defeat into a shattering victory. Since Marlborough England had never known such a triumph of arms. The public's regard for Pitt bordered on idolatry.

Pitt was not easy in his greatness. Throughout 1759 his relations with Newcastle were strained. He expected Newcastle to refrain from all criticism of military measures and to provide expeditiously the money which his plans demanded. Yet Pitt would not leave Newcastle alone to devise his financial measures. He had his own strange theories about taxation. He rebuked the Chancellor of the Exchequer in the Commons and denounced taxes introduced by Newcastle. He never hesitated to criticise either Newcastle or Hardwicke in words which were stinging, sarcastic and offensive. He showed the same lack of political sagacity in his relations with Bute, a pompous

man of little insight, who was the chief adviser to the
Prince of Wales whose succession, owing to the great
age of the King, could not be far distant. According
to the Prince, Pitt treated him and Bute ' as if they
were a parcel of school-children.' In this way enmity
was built up within the circle of power.

But Newcastle deserves far greater credit than he
usually gets. In spite of his own resentment and the
more vociferous resentment of others, he gave Pitt
loyal support, finding the money for schemes which
he thought so ambitious as to ensure disaster. In circumstances of utmost personal difficulty he gave Pitt
years of loyal service and made his conquests possible.

The ministry's difficulties increased with the accession of George III in 1760. George III regarded Pitt
as having ' the blackest of hearts; ' he insisted on
office for Lord Bute, and Newcastle's position grew
intolerably difficult. He was suspected by Pitt of a
lack of enthusiasm for the war. He was confident
Lord Bute was undermining his power with the King.
It was a moment which called for forbearance and a
spirit of compromise. Neither was forthcoming from
Pitt. For him there were imperative decisions. The
close blockade of France, the frequent and high-handed
treatment of neutral vessels which were searched for
contraband, the massive victories overseas, caused
Spain to fear for her own future. If France were to be
totally defeated, her own empire would be at Britain's
mercy and with Pitt at the head of affairs little mercy
could be expected. And Pitt no longer needed Spain's
neutrality. France's fleet was broken, her empire and

commerce destroyed. To Pitt Spain was legitimate prey. Realising the advantage of an immediate decision, Pitt pressed for war with Spain. But the Cabinet was reluctant, and the King and Bute resolute in opposition. For many months desultory peace negotiations had been in train with France. Pitt regarded them as a prevarication, but in this he was almost alone. The cost of the war was prodigious and the end nowhere in sight, so that Newcastle and Hardwicke were prepared to go to the very limits of diplomacy in order to achieve accommodation with Spain. This Pitt would not tolerate. " I was called," he told the cabinet, " by my Sovereign and by the voice of the people to assist the State when others had abdicated the service of it. That being so, no one can be surprised that I will go on no longer since my advice is not taken. Being responsible, I will direct, and will be responsible for nothing that I do not direct." So saying, he resigned the direction of the war into the helpless hands of Bute.

6

The Treaty of Paris and After

'PENETRATED WITH the bounteous favour of a most benign sovereign and Master, I am confounded with his condescension in deigning to bestow one thought about an inclination of his servant, with regard to the modes of extending to me the marks of his royal beneficence."

Pitt wrote these words to Bute within forty-eight hours of his resignation. Refusing a pension for himself, he accepted £3,000 a year from the sugar duties for his wife, who was also granted the barony of Chatham. He accepted these marks of distinction in words more obscure, ornate and slavish than those which he had used in the above letter to Bute.

It was an incredible performance. He knew the King hated him; he knew that Bute hated him. At once they used his acceptance of title and pension to blacken his character, and the press was filled with libels on ' Lady Cheat'em.' His friends and admirers were desolate.

Pitt was bewildered by the public outcry and wrote dignified letters of protest to his city friends. But Bute's exploitation of Pitt's weakness was too clever by half. Beckford stood by him and within a few weeks he was as popular in the city as he had ever been. He was received rapturously by the city fathers at the Lord Mayor's feast, in total contrast to the deadly silence of the King's welcome. The obloquy which Bute had attempted to fasten on Pitt by playing on his vanity rebounded to his own discredit. Yet for a moment Pitt's reputation had been in danger.

The fact that he could write in such terms and unthinkingly accept such dangerous marks of favour shows how remote Pitt was from the ordinary political world in which he moved. Four years of unchecked authority had confirmed in him the sense of his own sublimity. He knew that he had brought his country from the threshold of defeat and made her the leading maritime and commercial nation of the world. His mood was Olympian. In his very abasement before the Throne there is a quality of extreme vanity, and inverted pride, a relish in his prostrate adulation. That perhaps is why Pitt was so bewildered by the outcry which his pension and his wife's title engendered. In his gracious acceptance he was bestowing a mark of favour on the Crown.

No matter how much he might revere the Crown as an office, he had no love for its holder or his ministers and he was ever battering them with an invective which gladdened the heart of the city so that they willingly forgot wife and title and all.

At first Bute attempted to show that Pitt was not the only man capable of waging a successful war.

And Newcastle was soon wailing to his crony Hardwicke:

> " A most *expensive*, hazardous, uncertain expedition
> to the Havanna, when both ships and men are
> wanted elsewhere, a wild-goose chase (as I now
> understand) afterwards, after Mexico, St. Augustin,
> and God knows what, and the whimsical plan of
> expeditions going on faster than ever. Portugal is
> also to be defended at a vast expense.
> God knows from whence or, how? "

But Newcastle was even more flustered by the
rumour which quickly became a certainty that George
III was determined to bring the German war, and
Frederick's subsidies, to an end, even if it entailed
misery and suffering for his Hanoverian subjects. Newcastle hated the costly overseas expeditions which
burdened an overtaxed country, but he regretted
more deeply the desertion of our ally who had fought
almost single-handed the combined armies of Europe's
greatest military powers. Newcastle was consumed by
paroxysms of indecision. He was unable to oppose
the King and Bute on the fundamental issue—the
need for peace—because he felt its necessity. He had
long been suspicious of Pitt's untrammelled ambitions
and frightened by the mounting cost of the war, but
he deplored the methods employed by George and
Bute. In the end, he was driven to resign. Although
he did not know it, it was the end of his political
career. For forty years he had lived and loved a life
of breathless activity—managing, arranging, soothing

and securing majorities for Walpole, his own brother
and for Pitt; majorities which they needed to keep
the country's business going. History has been less
than just to his memory. He was skilful and adroit;
his view of foreign and domestic affairs, although
devoid of imagination or insight, was sound, grounded
as it was on a wide and detailed knowledge. His
destruction fractured the structure of Whig politics,
which, lacking his control, dissolved into warring
factions which made the immediate task of George III
and Bute easier to accomplish, although it prevented
them from establishing a secure government for nearly
a decade.

In spite of the flurry of expeditions, George III was
resolved on peace; and the ministry went hard ahead
in their negotiations with France, regardless of what
the public at large might think. Nor in this did they
entirely lack support. The burden of war was heaviest
on those who profited least from it—the squirearchy,
who paid the stiffest taxes. And what is more the
country had been at war with but a brief respite since
1739. War weariness was widespread except in the great
trading towns. And to everyone except Pitt, the total
destruction of the French empire seemed undesirable
—it would inevitably lead to a coalition of European
powers against us, in the same way that Europe had
so frequently united in the past against the overwhelming greatness of France. That was a lesson of
history which Newcastle and Hardwicke knew as well
as George and Bute. They were not against a peace;
they resented merely the terms upon which it was

offered. They wanted to drive a hard bargain; Bute wanted peace at the price he could get it. With the help of George III, Bute had his way.

France, too, was eager to make peace as soon as possible, for Choiseul, the French minister, feared that Pitt might be brought back into office. Negotiations were started in March, 1762, and they were rapidly concluded. Bute was able to lay the Preliminaries before the House of Commons in December.

Pitt was ill. The strain of the last four years had told heavily on his unstable temperament. After his resignation he had adopted an attitude of lofty independence. He let it be known that he had no attachments to party and that he was determined not to enter into full opposition to the ministry. But few believed that he would remain aloof when he was faced with the destruction of his conquests. And so the government regarded Pitt's illness with relief and turned a deaf ear to suggestions that the debate on the Preliminaries of Peace might be delayed in order to give Pitt a chance to recover. But Pitt was not to be denied.

Ill he might be, but he had the deep resources of strength which come to those who live constantly with sickness. He had himself carried to the House. Nor did he wish the Commons, nor the public that awaited him out of doors, to forget his malady. He was dressed in black velvet which underlined his pallor. His legs were swathed in rolls of flannel, and the vast boot on his gouty foot was much in evidence. Yet he was undeniably ill. His voice was feeble, and standing was so painful to him, that the House granted him the indulgence of sitting through part of his speech. He held the attention of the House for three and a half hours; at times the pain which he was suffering muddled his thoughts and he lost himself in involved rhetoric, but, again and again, the fire and passion flashed forth, ringing with the conviction which he was never to lose that the struggle between France and Britain was a mortal combat in which no compromise could succeed.

Pitt was appalled at the extent of the concessions which Bute had made. The West Indian sugar islands were to be returned to France; her trading stations in West Africa were to be restored; and worse, her fishing rights of the Newfoundland Banks were to be confirmed.

" The ministers," Pitt fumed, " seem to have lost sight of the great fundamental principle that France is chiefly, if not solely, to be dreaded by us in the light of a maritime and commercial power—and therefore by restoring to her all the valuable West India islands, and by our concessions in the New-foundland fishery, we have given her the means of recovering her prodigious losses and becoming once more formidable to us at sea."

Every concession not only deprived the country of the wealth which it had won through war but also weakened its strategic position in any future conflict. Furthermore, we had sacrificed in the most cavalier fashion the one ally of ability. By his exertions Frederick of Prussia had withstood the formidable armies of France and so prevented her from sending reinforcements to her colonies overseas and from launching an invasion of England. It is possible that, unaided, the British Navy might have so contained France, but Frederick rendered her task immeasurably easier. This Pitt could not forget. He had the highest admiration for Frederick, and he deplored: " The desertion of the King of Prussia, the most magnanimous ally this country ever had . . . is insidious, tricking, base, and treacherous." He could find not one relieving feature in the Preliminaries offered to the consideration of the House. After three hours' denunciation he concluded wearily:

" The terms of the proposed treaty meet with my most hearty disapprobation. I see in them the seeds of a future war. The peace is insecure, because it restores the enemy to her former greatness. The peace is inadequate, because places gained are no equivalent for places surrendered."

Worn out by his effort, he rested awhile to recover his strength, but pointedly left the chamber as Fox rose to answer him. There was nothing to be gained by staying, for Fox was certain of an overwhelming majority. Only sixty-five members voted for Pitt, amongst them his old loyal friend, Beckford, and Clive, the conqueror of Bengal. But in the streets of Westminster men were shouting for Pitt.

The Peace of Paris marks a turning point both in Pitt's career and in the history of his country. Since the fall of Walpole there had been a large measure of agreement amongst all classes who possessed property and power that the government's policy was the right policy. There was frequent irritation about incompetence in action or the incidence of taxation, but in fundamentals there was unity. After 1763 a deep and dangerous rift developed between the policy supported by Parliament and the policy which many men of affairs wanted. And as it pursued its dangerous course the House of Commons lost the respect of those men, who came to regard it as the citadel of a privileged minority, more concerned with their own ease and prosperity than with the welfare of the nation. Its actions were watched with a critical eye and the public was ready to accept, perhaps too easily, criticisms of its decisions. Unfortunately the government was soon involved in two crises of a magnitude which was beyond the naïve intelligence of the King and his insecure ministers.

While John Wilkes brought ridicule and disgrace to the concept of Parliamentary sovereignty, the first stirrings of rebellion in America revealed the total lack of foresight amongst the King's servants. Incompetence was revealed in every action. Pitt's friends looked to him for guidance and hoped that his return to power would save the nation.

But when Pitt left the House of Commons after his speech on the Preliminaries of Peace, he brought to a close the most significant period of his life. Never again was he to enjoy such authority or to find himself in a situation which made such demands on his singular gifts of detached application and strategic thinking. Furthermore, the unrelieved strain of these years had left its mark. The weaknesses of his temperament had deepened with the years. In the last months in office, he had treated his colleagues with unmasked arrogance. He could lecture a cabinet, but he could not listen to a discussion among his colleagues. The least criticism was liable to make him flare out with stinging sarcasm and scorn. His attitude became menacingly theatrical. His speeches, his gestures, his public appearances and private receptions were all marked with a monolithic megalomania which disturbed his friends and irritated his enemies.

Only in the heart of his family, at his country house at Hayes in Kent, could he achieve a time of quiet. There with his four children and devoted wife he could prattle happily in nursery language, and forget for a time the strange necessities which gnawed his heart. The devotion of his wife was remarkable. Never did she doubt for a moment that she was married to a man of singular genius. She did whatever she could to humour his whims and smooth his difficulties. She bore without complaint the estrangement with her favourite brother, George Grenville, with whom Pitt quarrelled in 1762.

On quitting office he had given up his London house in St. James's and sold off his carriage with typical ostentation. Unfortunately he had no serious intention to economise. The magnificent legacy of the eccentric Sir William Pynsent, who left Pitt his estate as a mark of his approval of his policy, had destroyed

what little sense of money Pitt possessed. His domestic
life was lived on the grandest scale. Postillions in blue
and white livery rode before him; armies of servants
attended his children; he landscaped his new gardens
at Burton Pynsent regardless of the cost. Debts grew
to mountainous heights, but Pitt was quite indifferent
to the consequences. Lady Hester herself shielded
him from the difficulties caused by his costly addiction
to the grandiose. All the ingredients were present for
fierce domestic strife, but it never came. She dealt
with creditors, arranged mortgages, and acted as
bailiff to their encumbered estates. She tried to build
up around her husband a world of self-indulgent
comfort in which he knew neither frustration nor
opposition. When the dark cloud of his disease
descended on him she nursed him with care and a
rare understanding, accepting his need for silence and
solitude. It was due entirely to her that he, a sick and
ageing man, was able to play a part in the political
life of the nation.

When Pitt resigned he did not intend to enter into
a factious opposition to the King and his ministers. At
the time of his speech attacking the Peace he had been
careful to underline the independence of his position.
He had begun his speech by declaring :

" Unattached to any party I am, and wish to be,
entirely single."

He believed that he could best serve the interests
which he had at heart by avoiding the usual manœuvres
of a politician out of place, and in any case he regarded

the politics of the *couloir* as beneath his new dignity.
He was willing to give his advice to any politician who
cared to wait on him, advice which sometimes lasted
for two or three hours only to be repeated with each
new caller. On one occasion Hardwicke hoped ' that
I might save him the fatigue of relating what he must
have been so often obliged to narrate. However, he
was not desirous of being spared that fatigue; for he
was so good as to tell me the whole, from the beginning,
to the end.'   At other times his aloofness irritated
Newcastle and Hardwicke, who were hoping to ham-
string Bute's attempts to rule without them by a united
opposition. They wanted this in spite of their suspicions
that Pitt might espouse the cause of Wilkes, whom
they regarded as a dangerous menace to the game of
politics.

John Wilkes, who was a protégé of Pitt's brother-
in-law, Earl Temple, had become notorious through
the publication of No. 45 of his newspaper, the
North Briton, in which he had been hurling abuse
at the King and his ministers for many months. His
paper was widely read in London, where his bitter
attacks on Scotsmen and his denunciation of the
Peace were relished. Wilkes had a brilliant journalist's
flair for sensing the trend of opinion. He loved publicity and enjoyed baiting authority. His deliberate
provocation of the government made it almost impossible for them not to take action against him. Also, in
the eighteenth century the press did not enjoy full
liberty, and many ministries had secured the arrest and
imprisonment of publishers of newspapers critical of

their policy without much difficulty. But Grenville's ministry acted rashly. The Secretary of State, Lord Halifax, issued a *general warrant* for the apprehension of the printers, publishers and others of No. 45 of the *North Briton*. General warrants had been used from time to time, but most commonly to secure men whose activities were dangerous to the State in time of war. Pitt himself had issued three during the Seven Years' War in order to secure men who were suspected of being spies. But Lord Halifax's use of a general warrant was somewhat unusual, a fact which Wilkes's quick intelligence grasped at once. He was arrested and lodged in the Tower. Wilkes immediately claimed privilege as a member of the House of Commons, for there was an immemorial custom that members of Parliament could not be arrested except for felony or treason whilst Parliament was in session at Westminster. Wilkes followed this up by taking out a writ against Lord Halifax and his messengers, sueing them for wrongful arrest and damage to his property, caused by their forcible entry to his house in order to arrest him. This arrest of Wilkes caused great indignation, particularly in London: it offered a splendid opportunity for attacking the government as tyrannous and bent on the destruction of the liberties of the individual. But it is doubtful whether there would have been such a clamour had the ministry not recently concluded their disastrous peace.

Newcastle and Hardwicke were perturbed by Wilkes. They did not like him, they approved neither of his views nor his morals. It seemed to them that adoption of his cause by the opposition would so disgust the King that their return to office would be made more difficult. They were immensely perturbed when they learnt that Earl Temple, with a full retinue of servants and coaches, had visited Wilkes in the Tower. Furthermore, Hardwicke had no doubt that the ministry were acting well within their legal powers and he was shocked by the judgment of Chief Justice Pratt, who declared that general warrants were illegal and laid down the excellent principle—when Halifax claimed the necessities of state as a reason for arrest—that there was ' no difference between state crimes and other crimes; they are all to be prosecuted, judged and punished by the same common and equal law.' This verdict was rapturously acclaimed by the London mob, who welcomed Wilkes with cries of ' Wilkes and Liberty,' a cry which was to echo in London streets for many a year. Nothing daunted, the ministry prosecuted him by name in the court of King's Bench for seditious libel. Wilkes, certain of his immunity by privilege, refused to appear. This was regarded as a new triumph and the adulation of Wilkes's supporters knew no bounds.

The situation was far less simple than it appeared to the public. Pratt was the great rival of Mansfield, an enemy of Pitt's, who had deserted Newcastle for Bute. And it is certain that had Wilkes appeared before Mansfield he would have been condemned. Also, Pitt disliked Hardwicke, indeed he tended to hate the whole tribe of lawyers, a fact which Hardwicke well knew. Pratt acquired great importance in Pitt's eyes.

He had proved a scourge for Mansfield and might be a convenient counterbalance to the oppressive authority of Hardwicke. Pitt demanded out and out support for Pratt before he would consider alliance with Newcastle and Hardwicke. If ever they obtained power again, they were to pledge themselves to give him a peerage and a seat in the Cabinet. On the question of Wilkes himself, Pitt made his position crystal clear.

" I know what liberty is," he told the Duke of Newcastle—an unpromising opening for the poor old Duke—" and that the liberty of the press is essentially concerned in this question. I disapprove of all these sort of papers, The *North Briton*, etc.; but that is not the question. When the privileges of the Houses of Parliament are denied in order to deter people from giving their opinions, the liberty of the press is taken away. Whigs who would give up their points to humour the Court and extend the power of the Crown, to the diminution of the liberty of the subject, I should never call whigs."

And the last remark was a good solid blow aimed at Hardwicke. Newcastle tried to avoid the issue by restricting himself to a hearty, but very general, approval of Pratt's actions. His evasions depressed Pitt, who could see little hope for the opposition unless it was prepared to adopt a clear and firm policy on large issues. However, Pitt was nearer to office than he knew.

Bute and George III were worried by the temper of

the country. The outcry against the Peace and the up-
roar caused by Wilkes's arrest convinced Bute that the
ministry must include 'names like a *Pitt* or a *Legge*
that impose on an ignorant populace.' The administration, too, was full of rancour and dissatisfaction, for
the great influence of Bute with the King naturally
bred suspicion and jealousy. The situation was, as
Charles Townshend described it to his mother: ' an
enraged people; falling credit; contempt abroad, and
suspense of all measures.' Bute obtained permission to
approach Pitt, and the sudden death of Egremont,
a Secretary of State, made this urgently necessary.

For the next week political circles were in a turmoil
of anxiety. Letters of inordinate length, written by
Hardwicke to Newcastle, were hastily copied so that
they might be circulated to other Whig magnates such
as Devonshire, who, as it was August, were at their
country estates. But no sooner were their hopes raised
by one letter than they were dashed by the next. On
Saturday, August 25th, Pitt had an interview with
the King, who asked him to draw up his administration
at once even though Pitt had made it quite clear to
him that Newcastle and his friends must come back
into office and that those responsible for the Peace of
Paris must be excluded. Pitt refused to commit himself
to names and spent the Sunday in consultations. The
next day, confident of his return to power, Pitt waited
on the King only to find that he flatly refused to
consider the exclusion of his own friends. George III
said briefly that his honour was involved and closed
the interview. " And so ended," Charles Townshend

wrote to his mother, " this marvellous transaction; conceived in a panic; submitted to in despair; repented of as soon as resolved, and finally broke off in a manner so disgraceful to the Court, and so ungratefully to the Crown, who has been made to confess the necessity of a change, and to stop equivocably at last in the execution of it, after so great progress and repeated approbation."[1]

Pitt was desolate. The prospect of renewed power entranced him. But once more his lack of astuteness in personal politics made him blunder. Newcastle or Hardwicke would have been quick to realise that a complete change of ministry could not be immediately accomplished and that it was unthinkable that George III should jettison Bute at Pitt's instant request. Nor did he realise that his loyalty to Newcastle and Hardwicke was repugnant to the King. They had always been ready to push him aside for the sake of office. But Pitt was totally incapable of the quick treachery which the situation demanded.

Nor did his loyalty pay. When Wilkes complained of his arrest as a breach of privilege at the opening of the parliamentary sessions in November, the Newcastle Whigs were ominously silent and only Pitt gave him support. Encouraged, the ministry secured a motion that privilege did not extend to cases of libel; after which Wilkes was expelled. In order to secure this result, the government had used contemptible methods; an obscene poem, the *Essay on Woman*, which had been filched from Wilkes's house when it had been invaded

[1] *Townshend MSS.*, Raynham Hall, Norfolk.

at the time of the general warrant, was used to blacken his character. Legally, of course, the House could do what it liked with its privileges and with Wilkes. That was incontestable. What was also incontestable was the restriction of liberty. As Pitt pointed out, if privileges could be so lightly cast aside, no member would be safe from the vengeance of a minister: all would go in terror of imprisonment: all criticism would be stifled. But members would not listen to Pitt and only a handful followed him into the opposition lobby.

On the question of general warrants, Pitt was more successful. This was a wider question, raising far deeper issues than the mere arrest of Wilkes. Pitt had been taken ill with a severe attack of gout and it was only with the greatest effort that he dragged himself from Hayes to take part in the debate which lasted for three days. Pitt was forthright in his condemnation of general warrants, regarding them as a dangerous threat to the liberty of the individual. He was excellently primed by Pratt and he built up such a formidable case against them that all shades of opinion rallied to him, and when the final vote was taken after an all-night sitting the ministry only just scraped home with ten votes. It was a great personal triumph for Pitt.

During the debate his sickness had been much in evidence. From time to time he had been forced to retire from the House. But Horace Walpole quickly detected a new note in his speeches; a new note of dignified restraint. His opposition was less sharply combative. He had begun to consider himself as an elder statesman, indifferent to intrigue for office, and reluctant to embarrass any ministry on questions of a minor nature. On the other hand fundamental issues were very much his concern. There he could bring his weight and authority to bear; and it was greater because it was more sparingly used. The conception of himself partly arose, too, from the development of his disease. From 1762-66 he was in a phase of manic excitement; his sense of his own power was sharper, although it was accompanied with great nervous irritation, bad gout, and insomnia. But his mood is explicit in his letters and the reports of his conversations, and it is implicit in all of his actions. Above all, it is reflected in his utter inability to act in concert with other men. He was prepared to patronise them; he was prepared, even, to insist that they should return to power with him, but they ceased to be colleagues. Men who had played a part in great affairs for the whole of their lifetime could not bear to be treated with such detached authority. They quarrelled with him or avoided him, not only Newcastle and Hardwicke, but also his close family friends, his earliest sponsors, the Grenvilles. Pitt bore his increasing political isolation without difficulty; it was consonant with his mood.

" As I have little thought," he wrote to the Duke of Newcastle, " of beginning the world again upon a new centre of union. As for *my single self* as often as I think it worth the while to go to the House, I shall go there *free* from stipulations . . . and whatever I think it my duty to oppose, or to promote, I shall do it independent of the sentiments of others."

In 1765 the King was finding the presence of Grenville and Bedford in his government utterly distasteful. They were brutal to his prejudices and indifferent to his advice. In such circumstances he began to scheme for a change, and Pitt's public reputation was a factor which had its attractions for him.

But Pitt's terms were exceptionally high, nor could he be moved from them although he was distinguished by a personal visit from the King's uncle, the Duke of Cumberland, who rode down to Hayes with a company of dragoons. Pitt wanted not only a change of men but also a change of measures, and he was insistent for the abolition of general warrants. But there were personal difficulties as well. Pitt was reluctant to work with the old Whig groups associated with Newcastle, yet he was equally reluctant to make his attitude clear, and Burke thought that the scheme was wrecked by his pride.

It was typical of Pitt's ineptitude at court politics that he should have lost the prospect of office at one moment by standing out for Newcastle and at another by refusing to work with him. Pitt's attitudes were always absolute but frequently inconsistent. The trouble was that for Pitt other men were mirrors in which he searched for the reflection of his own authority. He demanded assent to that sense of himself which was the hall-mark of his extreme vanity. Men as egocentric as Pitt can achieve great popularity, perhaps easily achieve it, if they possess gifts of oratory and elemental emotional power, but they fail at court and in the cabinet for their sensitivity is confined to their own needs.

When the King finally agreed to a change of measures and negotiated directly with Pitt, the breakdown was caused by Pitt's own brother-in-law, Earl Temple, partly because he felt that his own merits were not to be sufficiently distinguished, but also because he was doubtful of Pitt's capacity to carry on a government. He had noticed with alarm the growing instability of Pitt's mind—his increasing hatred of Newcastle; the resentment of any discussion of his own views; the need for isolation. To anyone who had known him throughout his life it was obvious that a mental breakdown could not be long delayed.

The repeated failure to achieve office in the summer of 1765 aggravated Pitt's discontent, and the fury which arose from the depths of his personality was focused against the ministry. For the next twelve months he was swept with waves of manic exaltation. As so frequently in the past the condition of world affairs was appropriate to his mood.

The Treaty of Paris sprang from a desire to avoid the costly burden of war. Much of the expense of the Seven Years' War had been caused by the extensive campaigns in America and it was natural that a man of careful and orderly mind, such as George Grenville, should consider that it was only fitting that the American colonists should be taxed to meet some of the expenditure for a war which, after all, had been fought in their interests. In 1765 he carried through

Parliament a Stamp Act by which all legal transactions in America were subjected to a tax. Pitt had disapproved strongly at the time but he was too ill at Hayes to make the journey to London and scarcely a voice had been raised against the Bill.

Protests in America had been quick and sharp, and amongst the colonists there was a general refusal to pay the tax. In the face of opposition the ministry wavered, willing to sacrifice the Act as an indiscretion so long as they could preserve intact the right to tax. But how to achieve this desirable end was more difficult to decide, and when Parliament met in January, 1766, the King's Speech contained no clear indication of the government's policy.

For some months Pitt had been at Bath brooding about the state of the nation, the folly of the American policy and the iniquity of the Duke of Newcastle.

" Faction," he wrote to Shelburne, " shakes and corruption saps the country to its foundations, while Luxury immasculates and Pleasure dissipates the understandings of men."

And he went on to paint the state of the country in the gloomiest colours and to denounce ' the dark creeping factions within.' This was a carefully drafted letter and Pitt intended its contents to be known. Not that he needed to heighten public expectancy; for months the correspondence of politicians had been filled with speculations about his future. And when he rose to speak on the Address on January 14th, 1766, the House was crowded to hear him.

The years had ravaged Pitt. He was gaunt, pale, lined, physically the wreckage of a man, but this only increased the effect of his words, which flowed with an eloquence and power that he had only rarely achieved. Experienced politicians hardened to all the tricks of parliamentary oratory, men with a lifetime's experience of Pitt's theatrical appearances were carried away by his amazing power in this debate. Without the glitter of his eye, the sweeping gesture, the rise and fall of his voice, above all without that mysterious quality of authority which he brought to all he said or did, his words lack the full impact which they had for his contemporaries. Yet nevertheless, they still echo with his fervour; they still inspire; they still challenge, for beneath all the rhetoric lies the belief of Pitt that law and custom must give way to the needs of a changing world, that rule by repression must ever fail, that societies like men are happiest when life is lived on their own terms.

The burden of his speech was the utter folly and absolute injustice of the Stamp Act.

" It is my opinion that this Kingdom has no right to lay a tax upon the colonies. At the same time I assert the authority of this Kingdom over the colonies to be sovereign and supreme, in every circumstances of government and legislation whatsoever. They are the subjects of this Kingdom, equally entitled with yourselves to all the natural rights of mankind, and the peculiar privileges of Englishmen; equally bound by its laws and equally participating of the constitution of this free country. The Americans are the sons, not the bastards, of England. As subjects they are entitled to the common right of representation and cannot be bound to pay taxes without their consent."

But Pitt reached his greatest heights when Grenville tried to answer him. Against all rules of debate Pitt rose to speak a second time and the House had been so profoundly stirred by his first speech that they insisted that he be allowed to continue.

" The gentleman tells us America is obstinate; America is in almost open rebellion.

I rejoice that America has resisted . . .

I have not come here armed at all points, with law cases and acts of Parliament, with the Statute Book doubled down in dog's ears to defend the cause of liberty . . . But for the defence of liberty upon a general principle, upon a constitutional principle, it is a ground on which I stand firm, on which I dare meet any man. I draw my ideas of freedom from the vital powers of the British constitution, and not from the crude and fallacious notions too much relied upon, as if we were but in the morning of liberty. . . .

The gentleman asks, When were the colonies emancipated? I desire to know when they were made slaves. . . . The profits to Great Britain from the trade of the colonies, in all its branches, is two millions a year. This is the fund that carried you triumphantly through the last war. You owe this to America; this is the price America pays for her protection.

The Americans have not acted in all things with prudence and temper. The Americans have been wronged. They have been driven to madness by injustice. Will you punish them for the madness you have occasioned? Rather let prudence and temper come first from this side. I will undertake for America that she will follow the example. There are two lines of Prior's, of a man's behaviour to his wife, so applicable to you and your colonies, that I cannot help repeating them:

> *Be to her faults a little blind,*
> *Be to her virtues very kind.*

Upon the whole I beg leave to tell the House what is really my opinion. It is that the Stamp Act be repealed absolutely, totally and immediately; that the reason for the repeal should be assigned, because it was founded on an erroneous principle. At the same time let the sovereign authority of this country over the colonies be asserted in as strong terms as can be devised, and be made to extend to every point of legislation whatsoever: that we may bind their trade, confine their manufacturers and exercise every power whatsoever—except that of taking their money out of their pockets without their consent.

Let us be content with the advantage which Providence has bestowed upon us. We have attained the highest glory and greatness; let us strive long

to preserve them for our own happiness and that of
our posterity."

For the next month, in spite of sickness, Pitt fought
America's cause. He struggled to prevent Parliament
passing the Declaratory Act which stated in unmis-
takable terms its right to tax America. Whether such
rights existed in law was irrelevant to Pitt, he knew
that a reckless assertion of principle was bound to
provoke the Americans. The ministry, he thought,
did not realise the risks they ran. He was keenly aware
of the vast wealth which we drew from the colonies,
for him they were " too great an object to be grasped
but in the arms of affection." Only by indulgence
could good will be restored and the disasters of revolt
avoided.

Although he failed to prevent the passing of the
Declaratory Act, his attitude to the Stamp Act,
backed as it was by the opinion of London and her
merchants, was accepted by the government. The
repeal was carried through amidst scenes of tumultuous
enthusiasm. Once again Pitt was secure in the affec-
tions of his London public; his reputation as a defender
of their interests was as high as it had ever been. To
them he was the Great Commoner, independent of
faction, independent of royal favour.

But, of course, the situation was not so simple for
Pitt. After all, he was a politician, he wanted political
power. He had seized the magnificent opportunity
which the Stamp Act had given him to bring home
forcibly to the King and his ministers the danger of

his opposition. And within a few weeks of the repeal he was letting it be known on what terms he would consent to govern.

" In England there are two possible varieties of ministry. One consists of men in favour with the public, the other of men in favour at Court. I have come to the conclusion that a combination of the two kinds would produce the best ministry."

He had also come to the conclusion that he must lead such a ministry. He rejected all approaches from the ministry in power to join them, and in April he retired to Burton Pynsent to await events. He had not long to wait. By July he was driving furiously down the Great West Road to answer the King's summons to form a ministry. For the first time Pitt was offered the sole direction of affairs, foreign and domestic. It was to prove a bitter fiasco.

7

The Fiasco

Pitt arrived in London, but after seeing the King he developed a hectic fever and retired to North End House on Hampstead Heath in the hope that the fresher air would restore his health. It was an ominous beginning. And it was followed by a sharp quarrel with his brother-in-law, Lord Temple, who curtly refused the Treasury. He suspected that Pitt wished to keep him in close subordination and surround him with cyphers. He retired in dudgeon to Stowe, sneering at ' that great Luminary, the Great Commoner.' This rebuff prostrated Pitt for two days, but did not deter him from his course of choosing men without any consideration for the strength of their influence. Gradually a ministry was assembled, a curious mixture of ability and independence, totally at variance with the accepted pattern of politics. The old Whigs, the Pelhams and Yorkes and their friends, were out, but the ministry contained many men of Whig attachments, from the brilliant and unreliable Charles Townshend to the negligible Duke of Grafton, soon to be the butt of the fiercest political satirist of the century, the writer of Junius's *Letters*. On the other hand the

King's friends were not totally proscribed; Lord Granby was restored to the Ordnance and Bute's brother regained his old office. American affairs were put into the hands of Shelburne, a young man of high intellectual powers and exceptional industry whom everyone distrusted and disliked. Such a miscellaneous collection had no natural bonds of loyalty, no common political experience to draw them together.

It was indeed, as Burke sneered, ' An administration checkered and speckled; a piece of joinery crossly indented and whimsically dovetailed; a cabinet variously inlaid; a diversified piece of mosaic; such a tesselated pavement without cement; here a bit of black stone, and there a bit of white; patriots and courtiers, King's friends and republicans; Whigs and Tories; treacherous friends and open enemies . . . indeed, a very curious show.' But perhaps more remarkable than the miscellaneous nature of the ministry was Pitt's decision to take the Privy Seal. At this time the Privy Seal could only be held by a peer; he was gazetted Viscount Burton Pynsent and Earl of Chatham. He had lost touch with reality.

Pitt thought that as head of the government a title was necessary for his dignity. And such a thought was the most singular act of folly of his life. He forfeited at once a great deal of public esteem. But it is essential to remember that public esteem was only intermittently important to eighteenth century politicians. And its rôle in Chatham's life can easily be over-estimated. There is no doubt that he was sym-

pathetic to the aspirations of London and her merchant
classes, that he could formulate their hopes in words
which made their future clear to them. There is no
doubt that because of this, his importance in the
narrower world of active politics was much enhanced.
There is no doubt that there were times when George II
and George III allowed his popularity to override
their prejudice against him. Yet in the last analysis,
his only way of obtaining power in 1766 was by
pleasing the King. His very attempt to do so was
bound to create distrust amongst his public—the
acceptance of a title was merely an added exasperation.
Furthermore, Chatham was well aware of the fickle
nature of public regard. It could be re-won as quickly
and as easily as it was lost. That, at least, the years
had taught him.

No, the folly lay in quitting the House of Commons.
There, by his oratory, he could achieve at times a
mastery of its members. It was his natural strength,
and Choiseul, the French minister, compared him as
a peer to Samson without his hair. Ennobled, the
Commons was for ever barred to him, and the House
of Lords was an alien place, inimical to his ideas and
to his style. " And to hope that he could win by it,"
as Gray, the poet, was quick to realise, " and to attach
to him a court that hate him, and will dismiss him
as soon as they dare, was the weakest thing that was
ever done by so great a man." In opposition, he
could never again be a threat to the stability of a
ministry, as the future was to show.

But for the time the King's wish and Chatham's

folly were one. " I know," wrote George III, " the Earl of Chatham will zealously give his aid towards destroying all party distinctions and restoring that subordination to Government, which can alone preserve that inestimable blessing, liberty, from degenerating into licentiousness." Indeed such a sentiment was consonant with Chatham's ideas and with the needs of his distracted temperament.

Since his spectacular triumphs in the Seven Years' War, Chatham's megalomania had become more uncontrollable. He had saved the country when no one else could. His far-reaching plans had been crowned with success. He had totally justified his use of power and so power was justly his. Men must unquestionably recognise his greatness. In such a mood he had lectured his last cabinet; and in such a mood he had lectured friends and enemies ever since; in such a mood he proceeded to lecture his new colleagues. " Lord Chatham," sneered Charles Townshend after a cabinet meeting, " has just shown us what inferior animals we were." In consequence he forfeited the loyalty of men of ability who expected their views to receive a proper consideration. Apart from rough old William Beckford who did not mind being treated as an ' inferior animal,' most of his friends found his manner unbearable. Yet Chatham seems to have viewed the loss of even such old friends as Temple without much distress; certainly such a loss did not make him concerned for the stability of the ministry.

Chatham was resolved to rule without party, without faction, almost, it would seem, without a cabinet, for he treated all of his colleagues as subordinate officials who were to receive orders and obey. The strength of the ministry was to be derived from royal authority and, if need be, the royal prerogative. Chatham had always venerated royalty, but in his diseased condition his reverence turned to idolatry. Naturally enough George III warmly responded to such marks of intense veneration which was one of the main reasons why this ministry of Chatham's lasted so long.

Secure in the knowledge of royal favour and indifferent to the sneers of dispossessed politicians at the youth, disparity and lack of influence of his colleagues, Chatham plunged into furious activity. For the first month of his ministry he was in a state of manic elation. He tackled at once the three grave problems which beset the country—the growing threat of the Franco-Spanish alliance, the increasing difficulties in America, and the problem of the East India Company.

France had in many respects failed to carry out the provisions of the Treaty of Paris and Spain, now her close ally, had never paid to England the ransom for the return of Manilla. Chatham demanded immediate fulfilment of outstanding obligations and backed his demands by ostentatiously sending emissaries to Frederick of Prussia and the Czarina of Russia, letting his desire for an anti-Bourbon alliance be widely known. With Chatham in power diplomacy might easily extend to war, and Choiseul acted with increasing circumspection until his worries were alleviated by Chatham's collapse.

It was not the fact so much as the implication of

France's failure to carry out her Treaty obligations which disturbed Chatham, for it demonstrated a new strength and a new confidence in France and indicated that she might soon be prepared to renew the contest for the world's trade. There were other signs too which perturbed him. France was showing a renewed and active interest in her possessions in the Gulf of Mexico; he feared that the French might take advantage of the growing discontent in the American colonies.

The repeal of the Stamp Act had been acclaimed with joy by the colonists and Chatham's popularity in America had been almost as great as in London. So complete had been the colonists' relief that they had scarcely noticed the passing of the Declaratory Act by which England maintained its right to tax unimpaired. But their enthusiasm was of short duration. Neither the enactment of measures nor their repeal could heal the breach between England and America, for the causes were deeper than contemporaries could comprehend.

There were two million people in the colonies in the 1760s. Only in the Southern states was the way of life similar to the aristocratic life of England. In the North-East, the focus of aggressive discontent, the economic, social and cultural life was dominated by liberal-minded, middle-class merchants. These men resented keenly the idea of subordination which permeated the attitude of royal officials in the states and of Parliament in London. They wanted life their own way; freedom to run their affairs and to mould their own institutions. They preferred to risk economic disaster, war, chaos, anything rather than remain in tutelage. They found the rein of British authority intolerable no matter how lightly held. In such a mood grievances flourished like weeds, and no sooner were they removed than others sprouted. Resentment was bred by the arrogant language of Governor Bernard, who required the colonists to recompense those who had suffered in the Stamp Act riots. A more serious grievance arose from the application of a new Mutiny Act which controlled the billeting of British soldiers. Some state assemblies refused to accept the Munity Act. Elsewhere rioters and not their victims were compensated. Even Chatham, sympathetic as he was to America, referred to " these irritable and umbrageous people quite out of their senses." Nevertheless, a policy was needed if the drift into anarchy was to be averted.

American affairs were the direct responsibility of Shelburne, who consulted Chatham on every move. He wished to pursue a firm but liberal policy. He was willing to draft a new Mutiny Act and to withdraw the hated redcoats to frontier regions where they would be more useful and less obnoxious to the colonists. Shelburne, too, was prepared to see that no obstacle was placed to the movement of the colonists towards the wide western plains, a movement which many British politicians opposed because of the danger of a further clash with the French in the Mississippi valley. Yet even Shelburne felt it was necessary that the New York Assembly, one of the most active and aggressive of the colonial assemblies at this time, should show its willingness to obey by carrying out the terms of the old Mutiny Act until a new one could be passed by Parliament. This last condition, which underlined the subordination of the colonists, would probably have wrecked Shelburne's policy, but in any case it was never to be tried out fully, for the rest of the cabinet was opposed to such an attitude to America, and before many months had passed Shelburne had lost control of American affairs. But for the moment, in the first bright brief months of Chatham's ministry, it looked as if American affairs were to be dealt with wisely.

The question of the East India Company was more difficult. In the days of Governor Pitt the Company had been concerned only with trade, and it was trade which Chatham felt to be 'the only object of their charter.' But the victories of Clive had changed the simple purpose of the Company which had become the master of territories greater than Britain, drawing a revenue of more than a million pounds a year. Shareholders in London expected vast dividends from this golden stream, but the Directors knew that much, if not most of it, would be absorbed by the costs of administration, but this did not check the outburst of speculation in the Company's shares, reminiscent of the South Sea Bubble. Then, too, the safety of the Company depended upon the protection given to it by the navy and the reinforcements of royal troops which it had received. By such action the government could be said to have established a claim to a part of its revenues. Yet no one could contemplate the confiscation of these huge revenues to the Crown, for such an action cut right across contemporary belief in the sanctity of private property, and moreover, as Chatham saw, " If the Crown seize them, through the medium of a House of Commons, there is an end of the shadow of liberty. English Kings would become moguls." Then there were legal difficulties. Many maintained that its charter did not give the Company the right to rule such huge territories. And there were moral difficulties. Dark stories were circulating in London of extortion and brutality by Company servants who were eager to get as rich as possible in the shortest time. Such corruption, if continued, many argued, would wreck the Company and turn its members into leeches, sucking the life blood from India. The final complication lay in the fact that many members of the House of Commons had interests in the Company either directly or through their relatives. And it was easier in the eighteenth century to act according to a frank self-interest. This grave problem could not be easily and readily solved; indeed it was not to be solved by any eighteenth century ministry, and Chatham himself wished to proceed with caution. He held the view that the ministry should take no action whatsoever until the whole matter had been thrashed out before Parliament.

The revival of Bourbon power, the unrest in America, the East India crisis, demanded all of Chatham's application and resource. After four weeks of feverish energy he collapsed. Nor was his collapse temporary; except for brief intervals of lucidity he was incapable of thought or action for the next two disastrous years. In the early stages he was able to go to Bath and keep up the appearance of still being in control of the nation's affairs. He was sufficiently lucid to make his views clear on both America and India, but he was unable to exercise his authority or keep the irresponsible Charles Townshend under control. Townshend, a man of great intellectual brilliance and a fine orator, lacked all political sagacity and he was determined to exert the right of England to tax America and to negotiate directly with the directors of the East India Company, both policies which were diametrically opposed to Chatham's.

In order to deal with the crisis caused by Townshend's attitude, Chatham, ill as he was, set out from Bath on February 10th, 1767. But the difficult winter travel was too much for his delicate state and he collapsed at Marlborough. Here at the Castle Inn he remained helpless for days, until he was once more spurred to making a further effort by the news that his ministry had been defeated in the Commons over the Budget; due, so many said, to Townshend's want of exertion. Travelling very slowly—often covering no more than ten miles in a day—Chatham reached London early in March and attempted to get rid of Townshend by promoting Lord North, but North refused to budge. This effort proved too much for Chatham, who retired to Hampstead in a state of mental disorder which could no longer be disguised.

Bouts of profound melancholia, in which he could not bear even to see his wife, alternated with acts of rash extravagance. At one time he planned to add thirty or more new rooms to his Hampstead house, for which he obtained his landlord's permission; at another he considered razing some neighbouring houses to the ground because they interrupted his view. A chicken was always kept on the spit in case he should fancy a meal. But there were days when he sat at an upper window vacantly staring hour after hour at the widespread countryside. He rarely spoke, and for months it was impossible for him to conduct any government business. Grafton was deeply pained when he saw him in May, 1767. " Though I expected to find Lord Chatham very ill indeed," he wrote afterwards, " his situation was different from what I imagined; his nerves and spirits were affected to a dreadful degree, and the sight of his great mind bowed down, and thus weakened by disorder, would have filled one with grief and concern, even if I had not long since borne a sincere attachment to his person and character." In the hopes of distracting his mind, his old home of Hayes, which had been sold after his inheritance of Burton Pynsent, was repurchased. But changes of air availed little and as the months dragged on there seemed little hope of his recovery.

It is almost incredible that Chatham should have been allowed to continue in office, but George III was extremely reluctant to part with him, and every time a more favourable report came from Hampstead, Hayes or Bath, he buoyed himself up with the hope that Chatham would soon be back at the head of affairs. The King clung so ardently to this forlorn hope because he hated the alternative which he might be forced to accept if Chatham went—the Rockingham Whigs. But the ministry had long ceased to be Chatham's and its policy was clearly at variance with all that he had said and done in his first few weeks in office. This was brought sharply home to him in the autumn of 1768 when he learned that Shelburne had resigned, partly because of his disapproval of the Cabinet's American policy and partly because of the ministry's refusal to resist France's occupation of Corsica. Fortunately Chatham was lucid long enough to see the danger of remaining any longer as titular head of affairs; even more fortunately he was strong enough to take the necessary action. In spite of strong protests from the King, Chatham resigned the Privy Seal and so brought to a close the dismal fiasco of his ministry, the strangest of England's long history.

From that moment Chatham began to gain strength; signs of his recovery had been apparent during the summer, for it was a clear indication that he was climbing out of the depths of his despondency when he had been able to discuss affairs with Grafton in October and afterwards to force his resignation on the reluctant King. But many months were to pass before his health permitted him to take a full and active interest in politics. As he struggled free from the horrors of his personal hell, he was confronted by the sight of his country in grave and dangerous difficulties. For nearly two years Chatham had been scarcely able to comprehend the drift of affairs, and what little he had understood he had viewed with the blank indifference of the insane. But as life and interest flowed slowly back, he saw his life work being torn to shreds by incompetence, misunderstanding and fear.

Even in the midst of his illness he was aware that Townshend was 'betraying him every hour,' but he lacked the energy and the lucidity to deal with him. Townshend had insisted on taxing America and in this he was supported by the Bedford gang who had been brought into the ministry in one of its minor reshuffles. In May, 1767, Townshend had placed duties on tea, glass, paper and a few other articles. The taxes were light—they produced only £40,000 a year and they could be regarded as external taxes in distinction to the Stamp duties which had been bitterly attacked because they were internal taxes. This distinction, of course, between external and internal taxes was over-fine. Chatham himself had paid lip service to it; indeed, he may even have believed in it; what is certain, however, is that had he been well he would not have countenanced these new taxes of Townshend's. But Townshend's action pleased many members of the House of Commons, who felt that unless a firmer line was taken towards America the colonists would become more truculent and aggressive, an attitude which had the King's sympathy. To underline Britain's mastery yet further an American Customs Board was established at Boston in an attempt to put an end to the widespread smuggling in which all New England merchants were happily engaged. Lastly, and fatally, Townshend suspended the legislative powers of the New York Assembly. Each action could be, and was, interpreted as a fresh insult and injury by the colonists.

But it was not the actions of Townshend's which were so disastrous as the inability to foresee their consequences. Resentment and rebellion were the inevitable results of such flagrant disregard of the colonists' susceptibilities. If insistence on the recognition of all British legal rights was the intention of the government, then such acts would have to be backed by resolute force. Maybe Townshend considered British forces in America adequate for the purpose or he may have misjudged the colonists' resolution and expected them to obey grudgingly a forceful policy. He was never to know the consequences, for, having imposed his taxes on America, this brilliant, unstable politician died.

The reports which reached Chatham at Hayes in the spring of '69 were deeply disturbing, strengthening his darkest fears for the future. The New Englanders were discovering a common purpose in their opposition to Townshend's Acts. They united to boycott British goods, an action which received support from many legislative assemblies, for which they were dissolved by the British government, an act which exacerbated the already bitter feeling in America. Throughout the colonies there was an irruption of incidents bordering on violence in which customs officers and the navy were involved. Open rebellion seemed only a matter of time. American affairs did much to arouse Chatham from his lethargy, but the case of John Wilkes proved a stronger magnet to draw him away from himself.

Chatham was well aware that neither in his gifts

nor in his temperament was he a common man. He
distrusted and disliked those who conformed easily to
authority, who accepted and tolerated the world as
they found it. He was drawn to the ardent spirits, to
reckless men, who challenged the world, for his was
a Promethean spirit. A fight, whether against the
Bourbons or a ministry, invigorated him and released
the pent-up force of his character. And the challenge
which Wilkes was making drew an echoing response
from his own heart. But there were deeper reasons
still why he should be drawn to support the cause of
Wilkes even though he detested the man and his
morals. In the darkness of his despair Chatham knew
the agony of the despised and the rejected, the misery
of the insulted and injured. This bred in him quick
resentment to all forms of injustice, gave the edge to
that furious rancour which was always bitterest when
it dealt with the oppressions of authority. The fact
that Wilkes enjoyed the publicity and clamour of his
squabble with Parliament had little relevance for
Chatham. He saw authority suppressing liberty in its
own self-indulgent interest. This roused his anger, and
anger improved his health.

The distractions of Wilkes and America inveigled
Chatham along the road to recovery, and once begun,
his appetite for life quickened. Hester Chatham took
advantage of awakening interest to bring about a
reconciliation between her husband and her brothers.
Naturally this fluttered the political dovecots and gossip
confidently forecast a new ministry involving the Grenvilles as soon as Chatham was fit to appear at Court.

On July 7, 1769, he was received by the King but no change of government followed. Chatham expressed his disapproval of the ministry's policy in regard to America, India and Wilkes. He let it be understood that his intention was to retire from politics. It is unlikely that George III wished him to return to the ministry for the King fully approved of the government's policy. And also, in Lord North, he had found a servant conformable to his ways.

In the first flush of convalescence the idea of retirement may have attracted Chatham; he may even have contemplated spending the rest of his days at Burton Pynsent in those country pursuits which proved such an anodyne amidst his young family, whom he adored. But a visit to Stowe for a grand family reunion of Grenvilles quickly dispelled this dream, and once more the intoxication of politics coursed in his blood. It was long since he had walked, a young man, in these wide gardens of Stowe, where nature was made urbane; long ago he had listened to tales of injustice and folly and all his ardour had been roused by a sense of his country's danger. Now, an ageing man, feeble in body and distracted in spirit, his triumphs recklessly destroyed, he felt once more the need to strive to save his country, to preserve her liberties, her wealth, her empire. He returned to London in high spirits and in fury. The fiasco was ended; the nightmare passed.

* 8 *

The Scarecrow of Violence

As SANITY and strength returned to Chatham he viewed the political world with increasing displeasure. Relations with America had steadily deteriorated since the government's repudiation of the more tolerant policy which he had advocated. The difficult problem of the rights and powers of the East India Company was still unsolved. Bourbon power flourished and strengthened without any protest. And an already dangerous situation had been rendered critical by the activities of John Wilkes.

Wilkes had been expelled from the House of Commons in 1764: the next year he went over to France in order to recuperate from a wound, received in a duel, and possibly to avoid the imprisonment which he knew was bound to follow if he stayed for his trial on a charge of seditious libel. Wilkes was not made for martyrdom. He spent a happy four years in France in congenial but expensive dissipation, waiting for a pardon which never came. Judging that the ministry might wish to avoid making a great stir out of a four-year-old scandal, he saw in the general election of 1768 an opportunity to recover his former popularity. There was grave discontent with the government and facile gossip about tyranny and oppression. The old slogan of ' Wilkes and Liberty ' became once more the rallying cry of the London opposition. The city itself would not have Wilkes as a member, but for Middlesex he was elected with an overwhelming majority.

The government had been aware of the danger of Wilkes. By fleeing to France he had become an outlaw and so liable to heavy penalties, but his outlawry was quickly quashed on a technical point. In this the ministry behaved wisely. Nevertheless Wilkes had to go to prison on the old charge of libel. That was unavoidable, for Parliament itself had withdrawn its privilege for members in such cases. Prison was no hardship to Wilkes. In the eighteenth century prisoners were allowed visitors and they were also permitted to make themselves as comfortable as their circumstances would permit. So Wilkes lived in great style, keeping an open table and receiving visits from the leaders of the opposition groups. Owing to the folly of the government, Wilkes in prison became a symbol for all, American or British, who believed that George III and his advisers were the enemies of liberty.

Parliament declared Wilkes's election for Middlesex void. He was re-elected and again the election was declared invalid. Again and again the electors of Middlesex declared their intention of having Wilkes and no other. To stop the farce of endless elections the House of Commons declared Wilkes's opponent, Colonel Luttrell, to be duly elected for Middlesex although he had only received a fifth of the votes cast for Wilkes. Naturally this clash between the electors of Middlesex and the Commons created an immense outcry. Wilkes's letters and election addresses were eagerly printed by the provincial newspapers. The rights and wrongs of the case were hotly argued by farmers in Cumberland and weavers in Yorkshire. The American colonists were as deeply stirred by what they felt to be a further illustration of the tyranny of the King's minister. Presents of tobacco and turtles were sent from the states to Wilkes in prison and he wrote to them that the colonists' cause and his were one.

The major support for Wilkes came from London and the great mercantile cities of Bristol and Liverpool, from those self-same men who had strongly disapproved of the Treaty of Paris, men who were worried that the government's American policy would lead to economic disasters in which they would be involved. Those very men, indeed, who had always looked to Chatham for guidance and support. The Middlesex election had taken place during Chatham's convalescence, and although he had been seriously alarmed by the turn of affairs he had been unable to give voice to his disapproval in the House of Lords.

Wilkes, America, the total inability of the ministry to see the disasters for which they were heading, made Chatham eager to take up the attack, and in this, too, he was spurred on by a private sense of grievance. For during his illness the ministry which carried his name had deliberately rejected his policies which in a sense they were pledged to uphold. This Chatham

regarded as base trickery for which he held the Duke
of Grafton and the King chiefly responsible. Against
them his mood was rancorous; it fed with delight on
the vituperations of Junius which were appearing in
the press.

These letters, probably written by Philip Francis,
are the most consummate political invective of the
eighteenth century. They were outrageously unfair
both to Grafton and to George III, but it is difficult
to withhold admiration for their boldness or agreement
with their essential aim—the defence of political liberty.
Certainly they were a joy to Chatham and he gave a
copy of one letter to his brilliant son, William, as a
model of oratory. The letters of Junius and the speeches
of Chatham have much in common; they both intoxicated their contemporaries with a sense of the
greatness of the English spirit which misgovernment
might confuse but never destroy. Junius aroused
intense interest and wide public approval, a further
encouragement, if one were needed, to draw Chatham
into the vortex of politics. He himself was eager. ' I
am resolved to be in earnest for the public,' he wrote,
' and shall be a *scarecrow of violence* to the gentle
warblers of the grove, the moderate Whigs and tem-
perate statesmen.'

' A scarecrow of violence! ' No epithet could be
more appropriate for that long lean body, battered by
illness and worn by time, yet still within this shattered
frame the old fires of rage could flame to intensity. He
was still capable of leadership, still capable of wresting
power from the incompetent hands of Grafton, and

bringing to an end the troubles of his distracted country. This, at least, he believed in the first flush of his renewed health, and he planned to subject the ministry to a vigorous opposition.

The difficulties of creating a united opposition were formidable. His reconciliation with the Grenvilles had given him the support of their small faction, but it was quite insufficient to create a serious threat to any government. The most powerful faction out of office was the Rockingham Whigs. This group was largely the old Newcastle-Hardwicke connection under a new leadership. The Marquis of Rockingham was a man of vast wealth but second-rate abilities. Fortunately for his faction he had obtained the services of Edmund Burke as his political secretary.

Edmund Burke is one of the most complex personalities of the eighteenth century. To the Victorians he was one of the greatest of political philosophers who laid down the principles of party government and made clear to subsequent generations the need for political institutions to conform to the traditions of society. Hence his disapproval of George III, for he maintained that the King, by exploiting the vast resources of Crown patronage, was destroying government by party and introducing personal government by his friends. But with greater knowledge of Burke's life it has become difficult to accept his attitude to party government at its face value; like Bolingbroke before him most of his philosophising had a keen self-interest as its basis. A broad ideological attack on the King's government was useful in attracting inde-

pendent votes and in gaining support of the discontented middle-class radicals.   However high flown his
phrases, Burke's immediate aim was to help Rockingham gain power for himself and his friends.   For
this reason he did not relish working with Chatham
to overthrow the ministry;   such an action might
too easily lead to the elevation of Chatham and a
subordinate position for Rockingham.   Chatham's
views on Wilkes and on the East India Company (in
which Burke's family were deeply involved) were
too radical for the Rockingham Whigs. In any case
Burke found it difficult to attribute any motive to
Chatham but a lust for personal power.   His intention was, thought Burke, ' to keep hovering in air,
over all parties, and to souse down where the prey
may prove best,' and he sneered at his ' significant,
pompous, creeping, ambiguous language.'   Nor were
the difficulties all on the side of the Rockingham
Whigs.

During a visit to Stowe, Burke extensively aired his
views on the iniquities of George III in attempting to
rule according to a court system, but his diatribes fell
on the unsympathetic ears of Lord Temple, who, with
Chatham, thought such a non-party government no
bad thing.   Chatham himself had always disliked
factions and parties and longed for a system of government which would transcend the pettiness and
intrigues of faction. It was not the methods of George
III which Chatham deplored but his policies, and he
wanted the Rockingham Whigs to concentrate more
on the enormities of the ministerial attitude to Wilkes,

to America, to India rather than on fictitious and theoretical issues.

In the first flush of energy after his return to active politics Chatham came within an ace of destroying the ministry. He did this by a display of forbearance alien to his nature. He deliberately forgot old insults and insisted that private animosities must be forgotten when the nation's danger was so great. In spite of ill-mannered snubs from Rockingham, Chatham persevered in his attempt to create a united opposition. A few of his old friends lingered on in the ministry and he set to work to persuade them to make a common cause with him. He was prepared to forget and to forgive their weakness in remaining in office after he had quit. Pratt, now Lord Camden, the famous judge of the general warrants case, and Granby, the most popular of army commanders, were on the verge of quitting the government. They were persuaded to await the opening of the parliamentary sessions, when Chatham thought their resignation would have greater effect.

The ministry had been made well aware that Chatham was to lead a crusade against them as soon as Parliament met. In a half-hearted attempt to avoid acrimonious debate the King's Speech was deliberately designed to prevent controversy. American and foreign affairs were but briefly mentioned, the outcry over Wilkes ignored, and most of the Speech was taken up with the disease which was widespread amongst horned cattle. Such a puerile attempt to avoid major issues came in for much ribald comment. Chatham dismissed the subject with irony and drew the attention of the Lords to the alarming state of the nation, but his speech lacked all force and fire, and Chatham himself was discontented with his performance. But whatever relief the ministers must have felt at this failure was soon dispelled, for Camden rose and confessed the error of his ways, making what was tantamount to a speech of resignation. He was careful to stress that, as a judge, he deplored what he considered to be the illegal and unconstitutional action of the House of Commons in declaring Colonel Luttrell elected for Middlesex.

This naturally brought Lord Mansfield to his feet, full of legal precedents and of fears of constitutional crises. Chatham had hated Mansfield for the best part of thirty years and he detested legal argument throughout his life; the combination of the two released the springs of his eloquence and the Lords were for the first time given a taste of Chatham at his most magnificent. First he dealt with Mansfield.

" Talk not of precedents! . . . I boast a sovereign contempt for them . . . There is one plain maxim to which I have invariably adhered through life, that in every question in which my liberty or my property are concerned, I should consult and be determined by the dictates of common sense. But to search in all the flaws of antiquity with a curious mischief— to run into every offensive crevice and to wind and meander and spin some silky line, entangling our plain sense, and defacing those clearly delineated ideas, which should be fixed on every man's mind and should direct his conduct—without which we can neither obey nor oppose with propriety—'tis insupportable—the English will never suffer it."

Having squashed Mansfield, he then set about the Lords and called them to their duty.

" My Lords, my Lords, let us not degenerate from the glorious example of our ancestors, who obtained from their sovereign that great acknowledgment of national rights contained in Magna Carta. Those iron barons were the guardians of the people. Yet their virtues, my Lords, were never engaged in a question of such importance as the present. Are all the generous efforts of our ancestors, are all these glorious contentions reduced to this conclusion, that instead of the arbitrary power of a King we must submit to the arbitrary power of a House of Commons? If this be true, my Lords, what benefit do we derive from the exchange? Tyranny, my Lords, is detestable in every shape; but in none so formidable as when it is assumed and exercised by a number of tyrants. This Middlesex case is laying the axe to the root of the tree of liberty. Let us save this noble, this amiable constitution thus dangerously invaded at home. Let slavery exist nowhere amongst us. It is of so dangerous, so cantankerous a nature, if it be established in any part of the dominions it will spread through the whole. My Lords, this is not merely the cold opinion of my understanding, but the glowing expression of what I feel. It is my heart that speaks."

At last the widespread discontent about Wilkes had secured effective leadership. Men of independent judgment rallied to Chatham and experienced politicians thought the days of the ministry must be numbered. Chatham awaited their resignation in a state of phrenetic anxiety. At first it seemed all too slow, but at last they came tumbling out—Granby, Coventry, Beaufort, and, finally, Camden dismissed.

But the Rockinghams were essential to him if they were to force the King's hand, and the Rockinghams still held aloof. With a rare display of humility Chatham went cap in hand to Rockingham and a formal, if uneasy, alliance was made. The opposition to the King was now formidable, and Grafton precipitated the crisis by resigning the leadership of the ministry. The gossips in the London drawing-rooms expected the immediate return of Chatham to power. Days passed and no summons came. The King was cheerful, obstinate and determined never to place himself again in the hands of Chatham. He patched the ministry with stop-gaps and persuaded Lord North to lead it. It was a clear indication that the King was prepared to make a last-ditch stand, but the pundits had no confidence in Lord North's ability to repel the combined onslaught which Chatham was to lead.

Chatham had great advantages. The wind of discontent was blowing furiously. Not since the days of

Walpole's Excise Bill had the country been so roused by any domestic issue as it was by Wilkes and his election. And this time the uneasiness went far deeper. With each passing year men had learned to think less of Parliament, to accept with a sneer talk of its corruption and of the relentless search for place and pension amongst its members. Seats for the smaller boroughs were traded openly, and as patrons traded seats, so electors traded their votes. It was all common knowledge, and honest hard-working, thrifty men thought the less of the government which ruled them. Many, too, of the middle sort of people had been touched by Methodism, by the great revival of religion which was led by John Wesley, who preached of the need for purity and honesty in all the dealings of men. Though many might despise Wilkes for the looseness of his morals, yet they admired his courage and considered his cause a good one.

The working classes, too, were behind Wilkes. Conditions were bad and the dislocation of trade caused by the peace had not been rectified. Low wages and poor harvests bred resentment. The newspapers, which were eagerly read by the poor, taught them to think of Wilkes as their hero and of Parliament as their enemy. They were willing and eager enough to surge into the streets and up to the doors of Parliament at the bidding of their leaders. Whenever they went abroad, George III was hissed and Lord North pelted. London and the great trading towns were in an ugly mood, a mood which experienced politicians felt they could use to their advantage, particularly the great men of London. And Chatham's old friends of the Seven Years' War, Beckford, Sawbridge and the rest, were all staunch supporters of Wilkes. They were ready for anything that might embarrass the government or that was likely to force a change of ministry in the hope of obtaining a change of policy more in accordance with their desires. Although their voices were lifted for ' Wilkes and Liberty,' they were concerned in their hearts for the trade which they feared to lose in America and with apprehension of the reviving power of France.

Chatham, sensible as he was to public opinion, was buoyed up by these waves of discontent. And he quickly discovered a note which went deeper than the old outcry of tyranny and corruption. Already men were asking themselves if Parliament could be allowed to continue in its debased state. Should it not be reformed before it became the despoiler instead of the defender of liberties? Chatham had always disliked the system of faction, the little political empires created by noblemen out of the rotten boroughs which they controlled. He had strong sympathies with the independent members who sat for the shires and the great trading towns. For him they were the sound part of the constitution, and Chatham came to believe that to save the country from a repetition of Wilkes's case their number must be increased, so he was to tell Parliament:

" The boroughs of this country have properly enough been called the rotten part of the constitution . . . these boroughs, corrupt as they are, must be considered as the natural infirmity of the constitution which we must bear with patience, like infirmities of the body, and submit to carry them about with us. The limb is mortified but the amputation might be death. . . . Since we cannot cure the disorder, let us endeavour to infuse such a portion of new health into the constitution as may enable it to support its most inveterate diseases. The representation of the counties is, I think, preserved pure and uncorrupted. . . . The infusion of health which I now allude to, would be to permit every county to elect one member more in addition to their representation."

These words were as welcome to the merchants and traders of the provinces as they were to the independent country gentlemen sitting on the back benches at St. Stephens. By his advocacy of Wilkes and parliamentary reform, Chatham regained all the ground that he had lost during the past few years. Once more he was fêted in the City and rapturously cheered whenever he appeared in public.

For the next two parliamentary sessions Chatham attacked the ministry with an eloquence and vigour which reminded old men of his first days in Parliament. For a time his age and sickness seemed forgotten. His words taunted the ministry and he lashed them with his satire, but they were also backed by the weight of a lifetime's knowledge. But the government did not crack under his onslaught and he was driven to attack the King personally in a speech which might have sent a lesser man to the Tower. But the government was too wary to make a public martyr of Chatham.

And many were not happy with Chatham's leadership. He lacked restraint. His whole-hearted support for Wilkes and his unremitting advocacy made more cautious men hesitate to support him, for in Wilkes they saw a dangerous demagogue. If Parliament gave up its age-old right to determine its own membership, it might be but the first step towards subservience to London, which itself was the victim of unprincipled adventurers. The danger of London dominating the King's councils was not a new one. Many had feared it at the time of the Excise crisis, now they felt it more acutely, and particularly so when the Mayor and Aldermen petitioned the King in insulting terms. Chatham, so it seemed to them, was furthering a rebellious cause and his championship of parliamentary reform was equally dangerous. About London there was much ugly republican talk and everywhere the institutions of government were held in scant respect. At such times the uninhibited language of Chatham was rash in the extreme. Many Rockingham Whigs thought the continued alliance with him of dubious value.

Also, the unity of opposition to the King was more apparent than real. Chatham, it is true, concentrated on the constitutional issues because of his own passionate belief that the liberty of the subject was in danger, but he was fortified in this single-minded attack because he and his allies differed on all other questions. The Grenvilles believed in taxing Americans; the Rocking-hams believed in the principles of taxation, but not in its application; Chatham believed in neither. Chatham wished to see a radical reform of the East India Company, but such a prospect appalled many of the Rockingham Whigs who were closely involved in its affairs. Yet difficult as these subjects were for the formulation of a common policy of opposition, Chatham might have been wiser had he attempted to use them. But both political wisdom and political caution played a small, intermittent part in his life. He loved battle: the ringing challenge; invective hurled without thought of consequence. In his great tirades against the Crown and its servants he found fulfilment for his own dark and strange necessities. He could not balance and compromise with judicious skill. All his attempts to do so had been lamentable. He had to go the way of his temperament even to failure.

And failure came. He insisted too much; too much on Wilkes and, perhaps more fatally, too much on the case of the Falkland islands. Our rights in these islands had been challenged by Spain. With great tact, and with considerable firmness, the ministry managed to deal with Spanish claims and preserve the British rights unimpaired. But this action of Spain aroused all of Chatham's hatred of the Bourbons. Anything short of immediate war he considered a lamentable weakness, due solely to the deplorable and decayed state of the nation's forces. Oblivious to facts he castigated the ministers as he had castigated Walpole of old, but peers were tired of the Bourbon bogey and refused to follow him into the lobby. As the session of 1771 drew to a close, it became clear even to Chatham that the King and Lord North were safe, that no matter how much the public thrilled to his words, the Lords and the Commons were indifferent.

He had enjoyed a brief Indian summer of vigour in which he made some of the greatest speeches of his life. For a time he was in tune with his world, fighting oppression, fighting for that mysterious liberty which he and the world needed, fighting to preserve the glory which had been his gift to the nation. But he was too old; he tired quickly; his disease was still with him, his body was twisted with pain. His rare friends, Beckford and Grenville, had died: Temple had quitted politics. He was alone with only enemies of his own generation. And the new men who held power feared this scarecrow of violence, so careless of consequence, so feckless in a dangerous and tumultuous world. By the end of 1771, it was clear to himself that it was over, that he had neither the strength nor the following to lead the opposition in its day-to-day contest with the ministry. He withdrew into a lonely and dignified isolation.

* 9 *

The Last Endeavour

As ever with Chatham, a period of strong enthusiasm and vigorous action gave way to lethargy and despondency. He was far too frail to sustain the efforts which two years' parliamentary campaigning had demanded of him. He was ill during the summer of 1773, and he viewed the world darkly. He told Shelburne, his one loyal disciple, that he thought Rockingham's attitude had ruined whiggery. Even the city was regarded with displeasure and he, of all people, accused it of a ' head-long self-willed ' spirit. But his bitterness was not all due to despondency and disease ; it had its basis in reality. A secret committee had investigated the affairs of the East India Company, an action which Chatham much approved. On the basis of its report, Lord North introduced a Regulation Act intending to reform the worst abuses in Bengal and to limit the powers of the directors. Yet this modest act was attacked with immoderate violence by Burke and his friends, who were deeply involved in East Indian affairs. Most of Burke's moral indignation was a cloak for a greedy self-interest which Chatham's long nose was quick to smell out. He had distrusted, and it would seem with justice, the talk of principles and party which tripped so glibly from the mouths of the Rockingham Whigs. Chatham himself was too exhausted to take part in the debate, but he made his attitude clear in a series of letters to Shelburne, who put forward his views in the Lords.

Chatham was distressed by the abuses perpetrated by the East India Company's servants in Bengal, whose desire to get rich quickly overrode all sense of justice and sometimes even of common humanity. Indeed in Chatham's view, India teemed ' with iniquities so rank as to smell to earth and heaven.' The danger, he thought, was too great a tenderness for the chartered right of the Company which gave cover ' to the most flagrant and ruinous abuses.' By these abuses we risked the trade of India, which to him was more valuable than any rights or privileges. Unless reforms were made, and quickly made, he feared for British trade in India which could only flourish if the Indians were free from bitterness and resentment. But Chatham's views had no chance of prevailing ; the East India Company had too many friends in Parliament, too much patronage which, used judiciously, created tolerance for its monopolies and abuses. But in his attitude to India, as in his attitude to America, there was a personal, emotional quality. Chatham responded warmly and instinctively to all sufferers from oppression. He was too close to despair, too near to misery, to feel any sympathy for the bland self-satisfaction of entrenched authority. Hence his mockery at this same time of the bishops who argued bitterly against the removal of dissenters' disabilities. It relieved his spirits to remind them of the poverty and humility of the apostles and contrast it with their smug and worldly arrogance.

But in these years he found it too difficult to maintain a continuous interest in politics. He was an ageing man and his frailties, physical as well as mental, were becoming more marked. Every speech which he made severely taxed his dwindling resources of energy.

Most of his time was spent down at Burton Pynsent in Somerset, interspersed, when he was strong enough, with visits to friends or to his married daughter at Chevening. He was devoted to his brilliant son, William, upon whom he concentrated both his attention and his affection. But there were months during these last years of his life when he was so ill that Lady Chatham ordered William to stay at Cambridge, fearing the effect of his presence on his father's unquiet spirit. Yet there were times when new distractions captured his attention and gave him moments of happiness and sanity. A lucky inspiration of his old eccentric friend, Thomas Hollis, led Chatham to take up active farming. Lady Chatham was soon the mistress of a dairy and Chatham himself plunged into breeding experiments on a bold scale. His animals he regarded as no common beasts and they were housed in palatial buildings at an extravagant cost. It was with relief that his friends saw his interest tire, and a sudden whim to have his old associates painted by Reynolds took on the air of economy. But soon he was back at his old hobby of landscape gardening

C.   K

upon which thousands had been squandered at Hayes and at Burton Pynsent. Not content with this, he set about his son-in-law's estate at Chevening, totally regardless of cost. This restless, distracted activity glinted with madness, a madness, indeed, which could no longer be hidden from the world. Gradually his illness was mastering him, dominating his life and destroying it.

In these distressing circumstances his wife played a noble part. She accepted his moods, his extravagance, his total inability to repress what he desired to be done. Her marriage settlement was consumed by his expensive follies; most of the estate of Burton Pynsent had to be sold to stave off the clamouring creditors. Everything that could be sold was sold and what could not be sold was mortgaged. She begged and borrowed what she could from anyone willing to give or lend. She lacked all pride so long as Chatham might have his fancies gratified. Her strength of will was formidably great, inherited in full measure by their favourite son, William. Yet she carried these burdens alone and lightly; in Chatham's presence all was tranquillity and indulgent love. She saved him from total collapse and kept a sufficient spark of sanity alive for him to play an intermittent part in the affairs of his country.

His wife's love could not keep away the dark melancholy for long nor could the febrile distractions at which he clutched. The world about him matched his darker self. His life's work was crumbling into ruin and men in power paid no attention to the warnings which he had uttered for the last ten years. Nothing, perhaps, could have stopped the revolt of the American colonies, for it was a movement whose roots lay far deeper than the constitutional or economic conflict about which controversy raged. The colonists were struggling towards a new society, free from tradition and authority. The vacillating policy of repression, alternating with moderation, had merely given the colonists time to convince themselves and others of the justice of their cause and to create out of the chaos of their institutions a representative assembly capable of uniting them in a common purpose.

In 1774 Chatham's health was sufficiently recovered for him to make an attempt to intervene in Parliament about American affairs which were rapidly deteriorating. The previous year had witnessed the famous Boston Tea Party in which colonists, decked out as Red Indians, had boarded a British ship and thrown its cargo of tea overboard, a demonstration of their abhorrence of the tea duties. Such a flagrant disregard of authority put the government and Parliament on its mettle. They acted promptly, but severely. Boston was deprived at once of its privileges as a port, and this was to be followed by the removal of offenders to Nova Scotia for trial, the quartering of troops in Boston and the suppression of Massachusetts' charter. Such intentions inflamed America and made many colonists resolve to resist if need be by force of arms. Every act of the British government they viewed with apprehension and alarm. They were infinitely suspicious when they learned of the government's

intentions to make generous concessions to the French
Canadians ; a deliberate attempt, they felt, to curry
favour so that in case of revolt the Americans would
be outflanked.

As soon as he was in London Chatham's health
grew worse, but he struggled to overcome his weakness.
The situation alarmed him intensely. He believed as
strongly as any minister that the British government
had full authority over all Americans. He was conscious, too, that this authority must be respected and
that Boston could not go unpunished. He was equally
aware that the actions which the government proposed to take would only breed fresh strife and might
precipitate war. But he alone realised that from such
strife France would gain immeasurably. " I would
have you remember," he told the Lords, " that France,
like a vulture, is hovering over the British Empire,
hungrily watching the prey that she is only waiting
for the right moment to pounce upon."

Although he supported the Act for the suppression
of Boston as a port as a necessary punishment, he
urged the government to go no further but to withdraw its troops from the town and to show moderation
in all things. But his was a voice crying in the wilder-
ness.   The Lords never responded to him as the
Commons had responded of old. Chatham returned
to Hayes in the summer with nothing accomplished
and with foreboding in his heart, but he resolved to
make an effort to find a solution to which both parties
could agree without losing honour.

As in his early days he set to work with a realism

that always seemed oddly at variance with his character. When dealing personally with his fellow-men Chatham was hopelessly at sea. He failed to comprehend their motives, misread their characters, trod without knowing on secret vanities, and never understood their utter exasperation with his behaviour. The presence of other men intoxicated him with the desire to dominate in which the alertness needed to manage men was drowned. But when it came to affairs, he behaved with admirable common sense. His vision was never distorted by his personal needs.

His competence in statecraft was never more prominent than in the summer of 1774. He realised that what was needed was knowledge. The government relied for its intelligence of American affairs on royal officials in the colonies who were one of the principal targets of American hostility and therefore prejudiced in everything which they wrote, and eager for the suppression of colonial insubordination. The colonists themselves were better served for they had Benjamin Franklin for their spokesman in London. Franklin was a man of intelligence and wisdom who was able to ignore exasperating minor issues and to view affairs from the angle of eternity.

Chatham asked Franklin to visit Burton Pynsent, and they spent hours ranging over the whole American problem and together they attempted to find some method by which the two countries could be conciliated. But Chatham was too wise to rely on Franklin alone. Thomas Hollis, who had a wide American connection, was asked to gather opinions. He obtained first-hand reports of the debates of Congress at Philadelphia, and information from Massachusetts, New York and Maryland. Not even the views of Mrs. Mehetabel Wright, wax-modeller and niece of Wesley, were despised. Chatham seized eagerly on all the knowledge which he could obtain; upon this he brooded and pondered until, with Franklin's help, he thought that he had found the way.

But proud, suspicious and a little mad, he would not share his solution with anyone else. The Rockingham Whigs were as sound—if not sounder—on the American problem as Chatham, but he could not forget the Declaratory Act for which they had been responsible. There were other minor questions of policy upon which he thought them unsound, but there were deeper, personal reasons why he could not work with them. He wanted the glory to himself alone. He was an ageing man. This would be his last chance to save his country, his last chance, perhaps, to acquire power. This he did not wish to share with young men knocking at the door of history, particularly Burke, who was distasteful to him. Nor were his closest parliamentary associates informed of his intentions; in his desire for complete secrecy there is a strain of mania.

He opened his attack in January 1775, demanding the removal of troops from Boston, an action which caused no undue surprise for this was the view commonly held by the opposition, but his speech was of his best; eloquent, dramatic and full of the invective of which he was such a master. But he realised that greater steps must be taken if rebellion was to be stopped and he spent a week of furious activity drafting a bill embodying the terms which he thought would secure reconciliation with America, terms which he had pondered during the long summer in the country. On the day before he introduced the bill he consulted Franklin on points of detail, but he replied to his first criticisms at such an inordinate length that Franklin gave up trying to modify the bill. He was wise enough to know that the bill stood little chance.

Chatham's bill was not phrased in the cold hard legal words of a statute, but glowed with the oratory of which he was the master, yet its provisions were clear enough and they were sufficiently liberal to make many, including Franklin and Thomas Jefferson, the great colonial leader, think that, if they had been accepted, they might have had a chance of success.

At first Chatham asserted rights which he thought could never be given up. Parliament had ' an indutiable and indispensable right to make and ordain laws for regulating navigation and trade throughout the complicated system of British commerce, the deep policy of such prudent acts upholding the guardian navy of the whole British people '; and the Crown must preserve the right to move troops wheresoever it wished in peace as well as in war. It is probable that these clauses alone would have defeated the bill in America, where they would have outraged men who were bent on revolution and lacked the liberal sympathies of Franklin or Jefferson.

But for the rest Chatham made great concessions.

He realised that the colonies must be granted those
liberties which Englishmen had enjoyed for generations
—no taxation without consent, independent judges
and trial by jury. But he went further than this and
proposed a constitutional solution which was both
imaginative and realistic. In order to achieve a
common revolutionary policy each of the thirteen
states had sent representatives to a congress at Philadelphia. Chatham considered this Congress to be
representative of American opinion, an institution, in
fact, of enduring worth. He pleaded for its recognition
as the constitutional link between the colonies and the
mother country. Hitherto each state had had its
separate channels of communication with the government in England which had been inimical to the unity
of expression, or of action, on the part of the colonies.
This was the boldest solution ever put forward by any
British statesman. It was singularly free from prejudice
and it showed imaginative insight by its realisation
that the constitutions which the colonists had devised
for their own government must be accepted. A small
loyal group of friends—Shelburne, Camden and
Richmond—supported him wholeheartedly, but the
majority made a mockery of his suggestions. Long
before the debate was over, he knew that his cause
was lost. Nevertheless, he did not intend to allow his
defeat to go without comment. He summoned all his
strength to castigate the ministry, knowing that his age
and authority gave him a liberty they dared not
question. After all, the men who sat on the ministerial
benches had destroyed his life work, and free expression

of his hatred and contempt took away the bitter taste of failure.

"This bill," he said, "though rejected here will make its way to the public, to the nation, to the wildest part of America; it will, I trust, remain a monument of my endeavours to serve my country . . . Yet, when I consider the whole case as it lies before me, I am not much astonished, I am not surprised, that men who hate liberty should detest those who prize it; or that those who want virtue themselves should endeavour to persecute those who possess it. . . . The whole of your political conduct has been one continued series of weakness, temerity, despotism, ignorance, futility, negligence, and the most notorious servility, incapacity, and corruption. On reconsideration I must allow you one merit, a strict attention to your own interest: in that view you appear sound statesmen and politicians. You well know, if the present measure should prevail, that you must instantly relinquish your places. Such then being your precarious situations, who should wonder that you can put a negative on any measure which must annihilate your power, deprive you of your emoluments, and at once reduce you to that state of insignificance for which God and nature designed you."

Chatham's periods of health and sanity were becoming pitifully short; the efforts of this session, following the feverishly spent summer, were too much for him and he succumbed once more to melancholy. Nothing had power to interest him, to draw him out of that dark lonely hell which engulfed his spirits. Under the strain his body, battered by years of sickness, was weakening. For two years the shadow of death lay across him, but in 1777 he revived once more to find his inmost fears realised. War between America and Britain had broken out in earnest and the despised colonists were showing ingenuity and resolution in face of the well-drilled German mercenaries whom the government had hurried across the Atlantic. France, realising that Britain could not easily extricate herself from her difficulties, had entered into conversations with American representatives to discuss in what ways help could be given. Since the Treaty of Paris Chatham had warned the country, time and time again, that as soon as conditions were advantageous the Bourbons would seek to regain their former losses. Time had proved him right.

The danger of French intervention was not a nightmare for Chatham only; the Rockingham Whigs, especially Burke, were alive to this dangerous situation. In their opinion peace with America at any cost was a prime necessity and they were willing to concede independence so long as our arms were freed for the struggle with France. To Chatham this was treason. America was the fountain of our wealth; the nursery of our fishermen; the foundation upon which the wealth and strength of Britain was based. He thought that America lost would bring ruin to England and leave her at the mercy of France. Yet he deplored the war, hated it, wished it to cease on any terms short of independence. Time and time again he told the Lords in his last great speeches that America could never be conquered. " You may traffic," he told them, " and barter with every little pitiful German prince that sells and sends his subjects to the shambles of a foreign prince; your efforts are for ever vain and impotent."

But the whole country was being rapidly converted to a policy of peace, and supporters of the ministry as well as men in opposition believed that Chatham's presence in the government was a necessity in order to convince the colonists that the ministry was in earnest. But most of the country had also been converted to the view that independence must be granted, an anathema to Chatham as it was to George III. In any case Chatham was too ill, too broken, to lead any government, and subordinate to North he could never be.

In the early spring of 1778 it was obvious that he was a dying man. The effort of his speeches during the winter had fatally exhausted him, but in April, when he heard that the Duke of Richmond proposed to press a motion for granting American independence, he resolved to make one more effort to thwart a policy which he conceived would ruin England. He struggled to the House of Lords where his appearance stilled all opposition. The Lords waited for him to speak in hushed yet embarrassed silence, for it was soon clear that his mind was wandering. Gaunt, tragic, Lear-like in his madness, his feeble voice stumbled from phrase to phrase, and for his hearers the scene was made more poignant by flashes of rhetoric which conjured the Chatham they knew so well—again he was before them full of passion, full of conviction of the imperial greatness of his country. It was the sense of shame which most deeply stirred him.

> " Shall a people that fifteen years ago was the terror of the world now stoop so low as to tell its inveterate enemy ' Take all we have, only give us peace '? "

That this should be the end of his long years of struggle was the hideous, haunting nightmare. Anything was better than subservience to France. Unable to continue, he made his final plea. " My Lords, any state is better than despair; if we must fall, let us fall like men."

He was carried insensible from the House; he was taken to Hayes, his favourite home. He dismissed his eldest son, sending him to his regiment at Gibraltar, for he told him his country's service was more important than weeping over an old man dying. But William was brought to his bedside, where he read to him from the *Iliad* of the death of Hector. And so his end was consonant with his life. Dying, he kept to the pattern of greatness upon which his life had been carefully modelled. He ignored neither style nor detail, conscious to the last that the eyes of the world were upon him. Parliament and the City were deeply stirred by his death. He was buried in Westminster Abbey with a pomp which would have delighted him. The City raised a vast monument in the Guildhall, for which Burke wrote the inscription, revealing in an inspired moment the secret of Chatham's greatness; the first statesman by whom ' commerce was united with and made to flourish by war.'

And so Chatham's career ended; ended as it had been lived with a conscious sense of his public audience. There is much to criticise both in the man and his work. He was arrogant, overbearing, proud. His policy brought war, and war brought death and suffering. But that was the way life was going, and all that Chatham did was to make clearer to men where they wanted to go. But his greatest virtue was his courage, his courage to endure; never to weaken to the very end in his strife to overcome the temperament in which he was locked. Like a great figure of tragedy, by that endurance, he reaches through to the hard and common lot of men.

Chronological Table

1708	Birth of William Pitt.
1735	Elected member of parliament for Old Sarum.
1739	[War declared on Spain.
1742	[Fall of Walpole.]
1746	Paymaster-General of the Forces.
1754	[Death of Henry Pelham.]
	Marriage with Lady Hester Grenville.
1755	Pitt dismissed.
1756	[War with France.]
	Secretary of State.
1757	*April.* Pitt dismissed.
	June. Re-appointed Secretary of State: Newcastle-Pitt Ministry.
1759	[Year of victories—Quebec, Minden, Quiberon.
1760	[Death of George II.]
1761	Resignation of Pitt.
1763	[Treaty of Paris.]
1766	Pitt created Earl of Chatham and Lord Privy Seal.
1768	Resignation of Chatham.
1778	Death of Chatham.

Sources and Acknowledgements

The Chatham papers at the Public Record office are the main source of Chatham's life. These have been extensively used by Basil Williams, *William Pitt, Earl of Chatham*, 2 vols. (1915) and Brian Tunstall, *William Pitt, Earl of Chatham* (1938), both valuable, detailed biographies. Since the first edition of this book, Mr. John Brooke's valuable study of *The Chatham Administration* (1956) has been published. My quotations from Chatham's speeches are derived from the sources given by Williams, except for that on pp. 19-20 which is partly taken from the notes of Sir Dudley Ryder in the possession of the Earl of Harrowby. Walpole's last letter to the King, quoted on p. 29 is from the Cholmondeley (Houghton) MSS and not before printed. Charles Townshend's letter to his mother (pp. 99-100) is in the possession of Marquess Townshend. The letter from Hardwicke (p. 95) is in the possession of the Trustees of the Chatsworth Settlement.

I am indebted to the Trustees of the Chatsworth Settlement, the Marquess Townshend, the Marquess of Cholmondeley and the Earl of Harrowby for permission to quote from manuscripts in their possession. This revised edition had the benefit of Sir Lewis Namier's criticism and advice.

The frontispiece is reproduced by kind persmission of the National Portrait Gallery, as are plates 2 and 3. I would like to thank the Earl Stanhope for permission to use the portrait of Thomas Pitt, the British Museum for plate 4, and the Dean and Chapter of Westminster Abbey and the Victoria and Albert Museum for plate 6. The portrait of George III is reproduced by gracious permission of Her Majesty the Queen.